C000228816

Social Media Marketing 2019-2020

How to Build Your Personal Brand to Become an Influencer by Leveraging Facebook, Twitter, YouTube & Instagram

Complete Volume

By

Income Mastery

Social Media Marketing 2019-2020

How to Build Your Personal Brand to Become an Influencer by Leveraging Facebook, Twitter, YouTube & Instagram

Volume 1

Social Media Marketing 2019-2020

How to Build Your Personal Brand to Become an Influencer by Leveraging Facebook, Twitter, YouTube & Instagram

Volume 2

Social Media Marketing 2019-2020

How to Build Your Personal Brand to Become an Influencer by Leveraging Facebook, Twitter, YouTube & Instagram

Volume 3

of the information in question by the reader will cause the resulting actions to be solely within his or her competence. There are no scenarios in which the publisher or author of this book can be held responsible for any difficulties or damages that may occur to them after making the information presented here.

In addition, the information on the following pages is intended for informational purposes only and should therefore be regarded as universal. As befits its nature, it is presented without warranty with respect to its prolonged validity or provisional quality. The trademarks mentioned are made without written consent and can in no way be considered as sponsorship of the same.

Table of Contents

Social Media Marketing 2019-2020: Volume 1

How to Build Your Personal Brand to Become an Influencer by Leveraging Facebook, Twitter, YouTube & Instagram

By

Income Mastery

WHAT PROBLEMS ARE WE GOING TO SOLVE?

Nowadays, it's hard to find someone who doesn't have a profile on social networks. This presence is even greater when the professional sector in which we move develops around the digital world. What we say or show in the different social platforms will have a direct impact on our personal brand.

Your personal brand is configured by different aspects that you will have to work on: professional presence and physical appearance; verbal and non-verbal behavior and communication; network of contacts; presence on the Internet and social networks.

Social networks, the tool to boost your personal brand

One of the key tools to manage and enhance your personal brand is through social networks. Used correctly, they can become the perfect ally to boost your personal brand. Although, if you do not manage your social networks correctly, they can represent a wrong idea of you or give future employers or clients a negative perception of you. To be able to project a positive image and to become known in your industry, you need to start by creating your marketing plan. The first step will be to start by defining your goals!

In which social network should you exploit your personal brand?

In order to define what networks, you should create a profile in you have to start by analyzing the objectives you have set, as well as other factors such as the impression you want to give people in your industry. Although each social network has its own peculiarity, when it comes to gaining visibility in our industry, there are some basic guidelines that you must follow and that are common to all of them.

- Include a profile image: Either a photograph or an original design as an avatar.
- Complete your profile information as much as possible: It will be the first impression that other users get of you. It may or may not determine whether or not they access your profile. Briefly explain who you are, what you do and link it to your personal or business website.
- Share content: Do it properly, generously, timely, intelligently, and consistently. And before you hit the publish button, stop to think if it's relevant and adds value to your profile. Keep in mind that your publications must be related to the industry in which you want to position yourself.

- Interact: Work on your online presence by conversing with the rest of the community, for example, connect with other professionals in your field. Share opinions, reflections, professional experiences or articles from your blog. Don't be afraid to express your opinion! It's the key to position yourself and to start networking.

- Monitor and measure: Even if your profile is updated, if you interact with the community and you share content, you have to start to analyze if you are achieving the goals you set. To do this, we recommend that you periodically monitor your profile, those of other professionals, as well as relevant content related to your professional field. There are Social Listening-Analytics tools that will provide you with these data. In this way you will be able to know which publications or content that you share is more attractive, you can research what other topics are being popular in your interest, you will learn who are your main followers, and so on.

Your personal mark on:

LinkedIn

It is the professional social network par excellence. So, if it's about positioning our personal brand, you can't forget to create a profile on this platform. In addition to exposing your CV version 2.0 and keeping it updated, highlighting skills and abilities that differentiate you from the rest., One of the tactics that will help you achieve relevance and visibility will be to write a good extract which includes including keywords.

And, of course, you'll have to stay active, interact with other users, share and recommend content. It won't do you any good to join a contact list if you cannot relate. Connect with other professionals and when you do, don't forget to personalize the invitations. Yes, we know you're lazy, but if you want that person to accept your application, show interest.

Also, don't forget to join groups with the same interests you have. This will allow you to learn and show your work.

Twitter

Twitter is a social network to generate conversations which means that you'll have to keep your timeline active. Not only should you share your own content, we recommend you generate conversations around other relevant topics such as industry news, etc.

There are tools for programming content that can be very useful in this task, but a recommendation: do not fall into excess when automating content. This can lead you to schedule publications that are inappropriate and very unfortunate with a sudden event, and that can make a dent in your personal brand.

The key to achieving visibility, highlighting your publications and generating conversation around a topic will be to include hashtags.

Instagram

Although Instagram may seem like a purely leisure social network, it can bring out your most creative side and thus reinforce your personal brand from a much more intimate point of view.

This social network can become a perfect portfolio to show your professional work with images and / or videos or simply to show your more personal side. In the second case, your challenge will be to find the balance between the professional and yourself, and connect this with your target audience. Take advantage of the closeness that Instagram offers for you to show your more human side. Now, close doesn't mean sloppy.

As with Twitter, the use of hashtags will allow you to reach more users and that visibility can be key to reach your target audience.

Brands increasingly use social networks to get closer to their consumers and generate a closer relationship with them. However, from a marketing point of view, we need to question if they are using these tools in the right way.

Let's remember that marketing proposes to get to know your consumers in order to satisfy their needs. That's why it's important to know what customers are like on social networks. In this way, we will evaluate the convenience of our brand entering a certain network and how to interact with followers.

The main uses in network marketing are to build a brand and loyalty towards the brand. It seeks to interact with the public, deliver relevant content and try to communicate with the company through opinions and by proposing topics. Facebook is the channel that works best today for this type of strategy. YouTube also works well if you work with audiovisual content.

DID YOU KNOW THAT...

- Pay attention to everything. Another important use of social media marketing is to promote and sell products and resolve complaints or queries from consumers.
- Microblogging Twitter is a useful channel for answering customer questions. It has high online interaction capability and the potential to generate "viral" content. '.

Despite the global economic crisis, the digital market evolves year after year, becoming one of the main engines of economic growth. The speed at which new technologies have been adapting has no historical comparison. While the radio took thirty-eight years to reach an audience of fifty million people and the TV took thirteen years, the Internet did it in just four years. The new media has catalyzed the emergence of innovative business models and organizations that, in just a few years, have become leaders in their respective sectors. This is a new digital revolution.

But, why is the Internet such a radical change in the way we communicate and do business? In order to enumerate arguments about the importance of the digital economy in today's society we could make an endless list, but there are some key factors that distinguish it substantially:

- ➢ Interactivity and connectivity without limits. We are witnessing the appearance of new mass media that allows multidirectional communication in a very efficient way, in real time and without geographical barriers.
- ➢ Versatility. The Internet is nothing more than a communication protocol, which allows it to be supported by multiple devices: TV, mobile phone, smartphones, tablets, appliances and of course, the computer. There is a dissociation between hardware and content so that users demand to be able to access their information from any device. Quite a challenge.
- ➢ Measurement of results. Unlike other media, the Internet allows us to accurately measure the results of any campaign or action we carry out,

through multiple metrics aimed at measuring, controlling and monetizing our objectives. And all in real time.

➢ *Transactionality* and accessibility. For the first time in history we can complete transactions in different platforms, this is what is known as e-commerce. You can look, choose, pay and you get your product delivered. This is done in no more than three clicks.

➢ Last but not least, the Internet breaks the traditional distribution model. It allows the distribution chain (and therefore costs) to be completely disintermediated, so that the customer-business contact becomes 100% direct.

Within this digital world, the e-commerce sector is expanding. It is a new electronic sales and communication channel that is growing thanks to the increase in Internet access, mobile devices, and new habits of demand. In recent years new projects have appeared in the world of e-commerce in most economic sectors that in a few years have become leaders in their sectors. This emergence of new competitors has forced traditional retail companies to have a presence in the digital world. New paradigms are necessary to succeed in these sectors.

And to be successful in this sector, it is necessary to acquire a series of skills and capabilities to conceptualize, implement and manage a business based on e-commerce.

Your personal brand on social networks speaks volumes about you.

Basically, its construction is intimately related to your credibility, perhaps the most important capital that entrepreneurs have.

Learn how to manage your work from your personal brand, regardless of the medium in which you work. Get to know success stories and access a guide with practical advice that you can adapt to your reality and make the most of it.

HOW TO BUILD YOUR PERSONAL BRAND IN SOCIAL NETWORKS?

Before moving on, to the treatment of your personal brand on social networks, I want to explain what a personal brand actually is. It is essential to understand this in order to be able to apply the general concept in the networks.

Deciding to work on your own personal brand or a client's one is a job itself. And this process begins with a general change of attitude in your life.

It's not a decision, it's a change. In this process you will have to get authenticity, be yourself, and show that part of yourself that makes you unique and different from the rest. That distinction against the competition, is which makes you unique, it is what is known as personal brand.

What is a personal brand?

Creating a personal brand is a succession of actions, such as creating, identifying, defining, designing, building, increasing, measuring and, finally, improving.

"Personal brand is everything you do... and everything you don't do..."

That's the best definition of personal brand. This is a definition of which the initial 50% is from the master Andrés Pérez Ortega. The second part of the sentence is of own authorship.

HOW TO MANAGE YOUR PERSONAL BRAND THROUGH SOCIAL NETWORKS?

Personal brand does not only belong to individuals, it also belongs to entities or companies have their own personal or institutional brand. In the same way, in the future you may have to manage a customer's personal brand.

When you are the company...

When you are the company, your approach to social networks should be aimed at your audience. More than 80% of people trust the comments and information of the people they know. This data tells you how important it is to have a correct approach to people through social networks or other online channels.

Tips for managing your personal brand on social networks

Display consistency in the image you transmit in different networks.

There is not much to add to this indication but, take the following into consideration:

- Portray the same image on all social networks and the web. This includes pictures, videos, what you write and the way you write it. All of this talk about you and adds coherency to your brand. (i.e., the same in all media).
- Address your audience in the same way on social networks and on your website, unless you use a social network with a marked age component or characteristics of its own that might make you think of using a more casual, or more serious tone. You should know better than anyone else your audience and what your personal brand should look like in every situation.
- If before you used social networks showing the wild side of your life, it's time to make a decision: evolve towards a more serious profile *(you don't have to eliminate everything that means a hobby or family, because we all have a private life)* or create a new profile with a professional image and leave the current one We would recommend for you to make this profile private. If your profiles had nicknames, not your real name, you're in luck. It's time to create profiles on Facebook, Twitter, Instagram or YouTube with a new and different look.
- Provides consistent addresses and information. Your profiles should all be moving towards the same direction, although it would be better if it were always the same.

➢ Create an editorial calendar that provides a variety of topics to write about. It should be a calendar of at least three months and, ideally, six months.

Find the right groups

Whether on Facebook or LinkedIn, you can join the right groups where you can learn, show your knowledge and expand your brand image.

On Twitter what you can do is create lists of people that you follow by sections of knowledge to have a good organization. Then you can eliminate those people, to compensate for the number of people you follow, and those who follow you. No one wants to show that it follows 6357 and is followed by 16...

Source: study lab social networks -

Personal branding requires constant effort

Building and maintaining a personal brand is hard work, and it should be treated as such.

Adapt your publications and content to your audience.

Choose the SSRs in which to be present (sorry, a negative for me: the social networks in which the audience of each one is located are not chosen, but are measured and it is decided where you want to be, always depending on the time we can dedicate and, in its case, the budget -our, or the client's).

Mark an editorial calendar. This is fundamental but remember that you cannot always stick to the script and that there are different types of news that need to be published immediately. Remember that Metricool allows you to use a scheduler for your social network publications.

Make exclusive publications for each social network

Facebook, Instagram, YouTube, LinkedIn and, above all, Twitter, offer agility that your website or blog will never have. Take advantage of that and create exclusive content for them.

On LinkedIn, in addition to publishing quality content, modify your profile regularly. In addition to standing out for the modifications, that will mean that you have new attitudes that your contacts will be able to approve.

As I said, do not limit yourself to publish on Facebook and LinkedIn only what you publish on the web. First, because you would only publish once or twice a week, unless you know how to easily create and adapt content. Second, because many followers are likely to get to know you through networks. Offer them something extra. Third, social networking publications are quite ephemeral. A link to an article posted on Tuesday will be forgotten on Thursday (or the same Tuesday if we're talking about Twitter).

If you offer different content during the weeks such as thoughts, personal anecdotes, work stories or individual reflections it will make your audience remember that you are there and what your essence is.

You can find out what networks your audience is present by accessing population studies that are easily accessible on the network. An example would be a study made by the INE or another institutes.,

Source *http://www.iabspain.net/wp-content/uploads/downloads/2016/04/LAB_EstudioRedesSociales_2016_VCorta.pdf* -

It is better to focus on two RSS feeds with consistent, quality content than to publish sporadically in six of them with content from other and minor articles.

Decide what you're good at and stay on those networks. You can be a better video recorder than a writer, or a better photographer than a video recorder.

Diversify content

I know I've told you before to focus on a maximum of three knowledge topics. But don't always treat the issues from the same point of view. Try to offer different perspectives and combine issues you are aware from different perspectives.

If you always write about the same topic in the same way, you will bore your audience, pigeonhole yourself as a knowledge giver and impoverish yourself as a researcher. In addition, you will cannibalize your own content, which will severely penalize your search engine rankings*.

We have to become storytellers so that what we remain in the brain of our audience. You have to practice that if you don't have it naturally. Try it!

Personal branding and social networks

Make good publications

This is basic advice, but. bear in mind that sometimes not even big companies do this.

Each social network has its own image formats. If you decide to create a publication with an image and a link, consider which format and size is best for each one. It's the same if it's a video.

On Facebook, YouTube videos don't look good if you put the URL directly. Download the file (*Atubecatcher.com*) and upload it from your computer.

Both on Facebook and LinkedIn, if you simply publish a link to an article on your blog (or another page where you've read something interesting that you want your contacts to be able to read), you should wait a few moments while the page previews that link, and shows a small box with an image and the first words of the text of that article. Then, you must remove the link to provide a cleaner and more professional look in the publication.

If this doesn't happen, you should make your blog available. You can do this by modifying the php code of the corresponding file in WordPress or in the tool you use for your page. It's easier to do it with a plug in, which can be ShrinkTheWeb (STW) Preview Plugin for WordPress, again.

Social Media and Branded Image

Study the influencers, relate and collaborate with them.

Influencers are people who have authority in a given field and who can help us have publicity.

So, meet them. List the influencers in your industry. Follow them in different networks. Visit their blogs. Find out about their projects. Follow them on Twitter. Send them emails. Ask them to connect to LinkedIn once you have completed one or more of the above steps. Little by little, when you feel empowered enough, share things with them.

Don't limit yourself to the virtual world. Go to events and network. Promote those events with your contacts. Talk to them. You need to remember to always portray a professional image.

Do not forget to take business cards. The perfect business card of the professional 2.0 should only contain the address of your website.

The personal brand is not only for social networks, it is your fingerprint and is present in both on and off.

Offers

If you want to build an important personal brand, you need to take your business cards and you need to offer your services. You need to be sincere when you ask potential customers what you can do for them.

The CEO of the well-known BeBee portal, Matt Sweetwood, believes that this is a sensational way to grow the brand. If you make that personal connection and make your customers feel that you care and that they are more than a source of income, you will earn them forever.

At your level, as an entrepreneur, you can start by offering yours services to your family and friends. Watch out, that doesn't mean you'll make your brother-in-law's company's website for free. But you can advise and participate in the marketing strategy of someone close to you.

Try to get into the habit of contacting at least one person a week to offer help and collaboration. You'll see it's not as altruistic an action as you think. You'll feel so good, I'd almost say its selfishness...

Start making questions

It's the best way to learn and get noticed. One question doesn't make you look like a fool. The other way around. An intelligent or correct question should be challenging to respond and   a great learning for you. Besides, that questioning shows you are interested in the needs of your potential customers.

Influencers and Personal Brand

Discuss. Debate. Talk.

Show your point of view. You're your brand. Without being disrespectful, charlatan or rude, you must offer your opinions.

 Just make sure that you do it appropriately and in the right moment.

My grandmother always told me: "You can say anything, as long as you know how to say it". I have it written down and read it from time to time.

TIPS FOR MAKING YOUR MARK WITH YOUR BRAND THROUGH SOCIAL NETWORKS

As you've seen, you have to act professional and transmit your brand through your social networks. Some recommendations:

Consistency be patient and go step by step. It's a strategy that takes some time. You must create a good network of quality contacts.

Concretion: Show your knowledge but remember there are different perspectives and you need to be able to see all the angles.

Work: if you've come this far, it's because of a job well done. Continue working hard.

Innovation: No one has ever written everything (far from it) about personal branding on social networks. Be yourself and chart your own path.

The last thing I'm going to tell you is almost the most important thing: treat well the content of your personal brand in social networks, but don't forget that each network belongs to its owner (LinkedIn, Twitter, Facebook, etc.). Although these lines have gone from your brand in social networks, I have to make you see that only your page and your blog belong to you and in them you must boost your MP, or personal branding, knowing how to make the most of the SSR. So, get to work.

 And you are going to leave a mark with your personal brand?

Social media marketing strategies: 8 tactics you can't miss

According to the annual report of The Global State of Digital in 2019 created by Hootsuite and We Are Social, 52% of the world's population uses social networks. This huge global audience using these channels represent a vast market opportunity for any company, regardless of its size. This creates an opportunity for you to create a marketing strategy which will allow your brand to reach more potential customers.

However, for your social media marketing efforts to pay off, the first thing you need to have is a strategy. Here are the basic concepts you should take into consideration when planning your marketing strategy.

Positioning strategies in social networks.

To start planning your social media marketing strategy, you first need to ask yourself what your goals are. Besides having clear objectives, it is important to have a differentiating element to position yourself in the top of mind of your consumers. s. If you do not have specific objectives, it will be very difficult for you to measure your success and ROI in your reports. Ask yourself questions like:

- ➢ Do I want to generate awareness of my brand?
- ➢ Do I want to manage the reputation of my business?
- ➢ Is my purpose to increase sales?
- ➢ Provide customer service?
- ➢ Increase traffic to my website?
- ➢ Perform market research to learn more about my audience?
- ➢ To be the leader of my niche?

Once you have set your objectives, these will be a guide to know what type of content you need to provide your audience, in what format and what are the best practices for your brand when investing in ads. Facebook Ads is a great tool to simplify and optimize this part, as the platform offers a variety of options customizable according to your objectives.

For example, let's say that the goal of one of your campaigns is brand recognition. These types of ads present the perfect opportunity to show the behind-the-scenes culture of your business and the team that makes it possible. However, if your goal is to increase traffic to your website, then your campaign ads will look very different and have elements like a CTA. Content creation is your job, but through advanced targeting options and tracking the performance of your ads, Facebook makes sure your ad performs at its best, reaches the right people, and becomes memorable in the minds of your customers.

Segmentation strategies in social networks.

As mentioned above, for your marketing strategies to meet their objectives, you need to ensure that your content is reaching the right audience. This is where segmentation strategies come in, a vital tool for your content to reach the people who may be most interested in your services or products.

Buyer Person

The first step is to get to know your audience, but you can also create a person buyer which is a great tactic to do it. A person buyer is a semi-fictional character who represents your ideal client. In order to create this client and make a profile, it is necessary to carry out an audience analysis to discover patterns in the demographics and discover the of your clients. Use social network analysis tools to extract the data needed to create these profiles. Platforms such as Facebook, Instagram and Twitter, among others, offer a free report with valuable information about the people who interact with your brand online, even if they are not your customers yet..

Thinking of the buyer person as a real customer will help you make informed decisions when it comes to crafting the right content for the right consumers. For example, Netflix is a global company that targets an audience with a very wide age range. On its platform, you can find content aimed at all kinds of niches, from cartoons for children, documentaries on planet earth, international dramas and award-winning soap operas, among many, many others. However, its content on social networks, particularly Instagram, has a clear focus on a youth audience. Coincidence? Although we do not know the marketing secrets of this streaming giant, this is probably not a random decision and it is very possible that it is the result of a market research where they extracted the demographics and interests of their followers in Instagram and realized the age range and behavior patterns of their followers.

Facebook Insights is a great segmentation tool to maximize the effort of your ads (and budget). Thanks to its segmentation features, you can target different audiences according to their age, gender, location, language, internet connections and interests. Facebook offers three types of segmented audiences:

> ➤ Primary target audience: thanks to algorithms and data collected by Facebook, with this feature you can target audiences that have the greatest potential to buy your products.

➤ Personalized audiences: target your ads to people you already know or have interacted with using the information you already have available.

➤ Similar hearings: new hearings combining personalized hearings with targeted Facebook ads.

Become an expert in the world of Facebook Ads. Make the most of your ad budget with <u>Hootsuite AdEspresso</u> or <u>Hootsuite Ads</u>, two powerful tools that make it easy to create, manage and optimize your marketing strategies.

The new era of marketing

Every marketer will be familiar with the marketing mix strategy and the four variables that make it up, the famous "4 P's of Marketing": product, price, point of sale and promotion. But are these concepts still applicable to a social media marketing strategy? Of course! You just have to adapt them to the online world.

Product

Whether it's a physical item, a service or an experience, the product is a key part of your campaign. Prior to the digital age, customers relied on sensory experience to determine product quality and feasibility. Currently, your product is your content and the format in which you decide to present it. For this reason, the quality of your content is vital and a great challenge. However, it is also a great opportunity, because within social networks there are an incredible variety of formats to present your product and highlight all its features. We explored this point in depth in the last "P": promotion.

Another element that has changed considerably thanks to internet connectivity is that customers can access the opinions and reviews of your product immediately and thus inform their purchase opinion. A tool that can help you to keep informed in real time of the opinions and feeling that is generating your brand or a specific product is social listening. Social listening is the practice of monitoring all your social networks to discover all the mentions of your brand, your products and your competitors. Through a single panel, Hootsuite facilitates the monitoring of these keywords and conversations in social networks. With social listening, you can ensure that your product always maintain a good image and join the conversations that take place around it. Hootsuite Insights is a great ally in this part, allowing you to monitor more than 100 million data sources and even track sentiment by location, language and gender.

Price

For many consumers, price is the decisive element that results in a purchase or not. The accessibility that the internet gives us to sell our products has reduced operating costs for many companies. Also, this has increased competition, no matter how small your niche is. In addition, users can compare your prices with those of your competitors immediately to inform their purchase decision. For this reason, setting the right price, which is attractive for your consumers and also profitable for you. This one of the most laborious and sensitive tasks of the digital marketer. Use tools like Brandwatch to always keep up to date with what's going on in your niche and with your competitors.

Point of sale

The point of sale is the place where you decide to sell your product. Thanks to the apogee of E-commerce (electronic commerce) and in particular M-Commerce (where users can make purchases from their mobile devices), any company can sell its products online, which has significantly transformed and simplified the purchasing process. For this part, it is necessary to do market research to find out where your consumers congregate in the digital universe. In this way, you will be able to decide, for example, if direct purchases in Instagram are viable for your company or if Facebook Marketplace fits your profile better. This isn't as complicated as it sounds. As mentioned above, the most popular social networks offer a free statistical report - like Instagram or Twitter Analytics or Facebook Insights - on your company's performance in these channels.

Promotion

Of the four "P's", this is the point that has most changed marketing strategies in the digital age. Often also referred to as "Advertising", this refers to the format in which you decide to present your product. According to the annual report of The Global State of Digital in 2019 created by Hootsuite and We Are Social, Facebook has an advertising reach (the number of users they can reach with their ads) of 82 million globally. Of course, this reach offered by social networks has changed the transmission and content of our messages completely.

To choose the best channel to present your product and meet your objectives, ask yourself questions such as:

Where do my clients congregate?

With what kind of content do I get more interactions: images, videos, stories, etc.?

What role do ads play in my content promotion marketing strategy? You can find the answers to these questions in your social network metrics and Hootsuite Analytics can help you with this.

Here are 5 specific tactics based on this information that you can implement in your marketing strategies in social networks.

Eight marketing strategies you can't miss

1. Present your content in new formats

We all know that images and videos get more interactions than a publication with text. Also, we know that stories are conquering users on social networks. Now, it's time to go a step further, get out of the comfort zone and use new types of media such as 360° videos, live photos, virtual reality and IGTV. HBO is one of the companies that has used some of these new immersive formats in their favor, just as they did in their different campaigns of the successful TV series "Game of Thrones".

360° Videos

VR

IGTV

One of the greatest incentives of the digital age is the possibility of taking advantage of technological advances for your benefit.

2. Use similar audiences in your marketing strategies

The tool of similar audiences is a great ally to find new clients. The platform is based on the characteristics of your target audience (the customers you have already interacted with) to find new prospects, integrate them into your sales funnel and thus improve the performance of your ads.

Similar audiences on Facebook, for example, are based on different target audiences (or seed audiences) depending on the goal you want to achieve. For example, if your goal is to increase your sales, Facebook will be guided by the customers who have visited your website the most.

To extract valuable information from this practice, you need to test with different audiences and measure their performance. Which works best for you? Find out how to build a family audience with the Facebook Ad Manager.

With Hootsuite Ads, you can control all your ads from a single platform.

3. A/B testing to optimize your content and marketing strategies

A/B tests are a super valuable research tool for testing small variations in your advertising content to determine which is most effective for your target audience. For example: you are about to launch a new product and you are planning the campaign. However, you're not sure if a video ad or a photo ad is best for your audience, or you have two copies to accompany your image and you don't know which one to use. An A/B test allows you to test the two different types of ads and measure the results across different variables to find out in which format you are most likely to interact with your customers.

Over time, you'll get information that will help you tailor your content for each social network and for each specific audience, which will help you refine your social media marketing strategy.

4. Check the performance of your marketing strategy.

It's time to create your monthly report: how do you verify that your marketing strategies are paying off? These two tools will be of great help:

Facebook Pixel

The Facebook pixel is a snippet of code that you can install on your website to track the actions users took on your page after viewing a Facebook ad.

With cookies that track interactions with your customers, Facebook Pixel helps ensure that your ads are seen by the people most likely to take the action you want. The great advantage of this is that it allows you to improve your ad conversion rate (i.e., know if your ads are really getting the customer to take action) and get a better return on investment. This code also works to optimize your ads and build audiences.

In the Facebook for Business blog, the platform recorded the success story of Columbia Central University located in Puerto Rico when it launched a conversion campaign focused on generating more subscriptions from new students with the help of the pixel. The campaign consisted of videos and images displayed on Facebook that reflected school life within the university and the Facebook Pixel helped them segment the audience to reach new customers and measure conversions on the institution's website and then re-promote their ads to similar audiences.

(Source: Facebook for companies)

These were the numbers they got:

> ➤ 71% increase in prospectus acquisition
> ➤ 80% increase in website traffic
> ➤ 12X return on investment

Check out our complete Facebook Pixel guide and start using it today.

Hootsuite Analytics

With Hootsuite Analytics, you can visualize detailed reports with tangible and quantifiable data. With this analysis tool you can measure the success of your campaigns and marketing strategies in real time without having to review the Analytics report of each social network separately. With easy-to-use dashboards and the option to create an unlimited number of reports, you can analyze metrics such as publications, followers, interactions and traffic from platforms like Facebook, Twitter and Instagram in one place. That way, you'll know what's working, what you need to improve, and where to focus your budget.

5.   Stay creative and up to date

The world of digital marketing and social networks is a space in constant evolution, so it is essential to stay at the forefront of everything that is happening in this microcosm.

To know the most relevant news of the advertising industry in your day to day, configure an RSS reader as Feedly or Syndicator Pro of Hootsuite to monitor in real time the latest publications of sites such as Merca 2.0, Adweek and, of course, the Hootsuite blog. This will save you a lot of time, as you won't have to visit each website individually and check its content.

Also, it is important that you continue your education. In our list of online community manager courses, you'll find options to stimulate your creativity, improve your content editing and become an expert on Facebook Ads and branding.

6. Promote your content on all your platforms (Cross promotion)

One of the easiest marketing strategies to implement is cross promotion. Imagine you're trying to grow your YouTube channel, but you're not having much success at the moment and decide to post a link to your video on Facebook. Publishing that link is the first step in your cross promotion. Either way, there is a lot more to do and some practices that you can follow to improve the performance of this strategy.

Cross-promotion depends on two elements, the "hero" content and the support content. Hero content is that piece of content that you've invested the most time in and it's the content where you want your marketing strategy to focus its results. Supporting content is the publications that will promote your "great content" on other platforms.

Returning to the YouTube example, your hero content would be your video and your supporting content would be the Instagram stories, Facebook publications, etc., which will support the promotion of your video.

Create publications specific to each social platform to promote your hero content.

Cross-promotion is not about posting the same message on all platforms hoping that it brings traffic to your hero content. The idea is to adapt the message so that it contributes to the conversation of that network.

(Source: DonutMedia Instagram)

Both refer to their hero content on YouTube. However, they do so with content   on Instagram and following the best practices of the platform. In the first one we can observe a traditional publication, without calls to action or other texts that may distract from the content of the image. It is not until the description, where the hero content is discussed, and its audience is invited to watch the video. This is very different from publishing the video hero's thumbnail on Instagram and expecting it to bring traffic to your website. Unfortunately, it's a practice I've seen with many youtubers.

Why should you create specific content in Instagram? ... or any other network.

Interaction rates in Instagram drop drastically when the image has superimposed text, so a publication specific to this platform will have better interaction and lead more people to your hero content.

Similarly, Instagram stories are a key tool in your social media marketing strategy.

(Source: DonutMedia Instagram)

In this example from <u>Donut Media</u>, he is using the stories to promote a video from his YouTube channel. Either way, they are doing it by creating a native video to the platform, with the right proportions, time limits and other considerations.

7. Optimize your content on each platform

If you want your content to have greater reach, you will have to optimize it using the best practices of the social platform where you want to publish it. For example, I mean that if you publish a video on YouTube make sure you add the most relevant tags to its content, use no more than 70 characters in its title to attract the attention of your followers (this is the maximum limit visible in mobile searches), etc..

If you want to learn how to optimize your content on social networks, I recommend you look for video tutorials to optimize your content on each social network.

Each social network has optimization rules and "best practices". I have put the practices in inverted commas because if you don't follow them your organic reach will be affected; therefore, they are not so much recommendations but requirements. Another example of this is <u>Facebook's 20%</u> rule, with which images covered in text in 20% of their total area or more will be negatively affected by Facebook's algorithm, their organic distribution will be reduced and they cannot be promoted.

(Source: Facebook)

In the following case Facebook determined that the text corresponded to less than 20% of the image, so it will be possible to promote it, anyway, its performance will be lower because the text occupies a larger percentage of what Facebook would consider optimal for its platform. Our recommendation: keep the text to a minimum.

(Source: Facebook)

8. Create a community of super fans and brand ambassadors

Finally, the most important step in your social media marketing strategy is going to be to create a community of super fans or brand ambassadors. These are people who follow your content, interact with it on a regular basis and are interested in representing your brand, channel or fan community on social networks.

Building a community of ambassadors will allow you to strengthen your marketing strategy for the organic distribution of your content. Every time you publish a new video, photo or any other type of content, you are ensuring that it will be shared organically with social circles outside your area of influence, circles that you will try to acquire.

Remember that this is a reciprocal relationship and that you are going to have to offer greater value to this community than to the rest of your followers. One way to show your appreciation could be by sending them small gifts, mentioning them in your publications or even a direct, personal message can be very valuable.

Categories ' Social Media Data and Statistics

Welcome to our Social Network Data and Statistics section! The articles you will find here deal with a very important aspect for those of us who work at Social Media, as thanks to this information we can channel communication investments to get the most out of them.

What is the purpose of Social Network Data and Statistics?

There are very good reasons why Marketers, Community Managers, Social Media Managers and everyone who works with Social Networks should take Statistics into account when performing their online tasks. Here are the five most important ones:

1- They Serve You to Know Your Audience on Social Networks

As you know, it is essential to know who you are addressing in order to design the most accurate messages possible. For example, if your target audience is people over 50, then it is advisable to avoid the idioms of teenagers or much younger people.

Thanks to tools such as Google Analytics or Facebook Insights, you can know the origin of the people who visit your social accounts or your site, which pages they come from, which sections they navigate, for how long and other valuable data to optimize your site, your proposals and your publications.

2- They help you to measure the impact of your actions on your audience.

Social Network Statistics are essential to gradually improve the quality of your Social Media publications. With their help you can analyze which contents your followers like the most, or at which times you get a greater amount of responses from the public.

Normally all social platforms offer you statistical data about your accounts, including Instagram, which recently implemented that and other updates. Therefore, there are a number of Social Network Statistics that every Community Manager should be able to read yes or yes.

3- Let You Decide Where to Direct Your Communication Efforts

From Social Network Statistics you can channel your investment (time, money, work) in Social Media in the best way. It so happens that this information is essential to determine the profitability of certain stocks. For example, if you discover that your audience is mostly young you will be able to adapt your content for them.

If you don't know the demographics of your audience, your publications may not be as effective. In this sense, segmentation is an essential step in achieving the best results possible which can only be achieved by getting information from your audience (i.e., through statistics).

4- Enable You to Know How Close You Are to Achieving Your Goals

To find out if your online activities help you effectively to achieve your marketing goals, there are two fundamental steps. One of them is to record your Social Media strategy in writing (i.e., document your actions in Social Media), in order to plan and execute your communications in an orderly manner.

The other instance to check if your content marketing strategies are working is to check your social network statistics. They help you to know basic questions such as how many people have seen each of your publications, in order to guide the type of content you share according to "what you have seen the most".

5- Function as a Guide to Knowing the Terrain Where You Will Work

In addition to Social Media statistics related to your particular accounts, it is very important to know the Social Media situation before making decisions about your online strategies. Aspects such as the type of audience and the contents on which the Networks focus are essential to decide which ones to invest in.

For example, if you have a women's clothing store or an interior decorating house, you will surely be interested in investing in Pinterest, depending on what its statistics show: 85% of its users are women. For its part, Facebook is a must, as it is the most widespread platform (with more than a billion users).

Data and statistics that the Community Manager should monitor and present in its Results Reports.

> To find out how effective your *Social Media* performance is, there are *Social Network statistics*. Analyzing such data is the best way to know if you are reaching your *digital marketing* goals, or if it is time to make a shift in your strategy. That's why today I'll share information about *which Social Network statistics a Community Manager should be able to read. Here we go!*

Social Network Statistics: which are the most important?

As we said above, *Social Network statistics* are really useful: they let you know if you are effectively reaching your audience and help you choose the best content to share. Now, each of your social accounts includes its own metrics, and you need to know which are the most important to measure the success of your campaigns. For this reason, I will share with you below the determining metrics of each Social Network.

Facebook Insights

Facebook statistics are known as Facebook Insights, and you can find them in the bar at the top of your Fan Page.

The data provided by Facebook statistics includes the metrics for each of your posts, your followers and the reach of each of your posts. You can also establish a list of pages about which you would like to receive analytics. The main parameters you should pay attention to in relation to Facebook Insights are:

- ➤ Scope: indicates how many people have seen your publication.
- ➤ Comments: indicate how many comments your post has received.
- ➤ Likes: shows the number of people who liked your publication.

- ➢ Clicks in posts indicate how many times users have clicked on your posts, discarding Likes and shared.
- ➢ Times it was shared: Shows the number of times your post was shared.

Statistics on Twitter

You can view your statistics on Twitter through Twitter Analytics. There you have the possibility to obtain information about the performance of your account during the last 28 days. Among the most interesting data offered by this service is the number of impressions of each of your tweets, which reveals the effective reach that each of your posts had in terms of users. Twitter also gives you the opportunity to view individual statistics for each publication. For this you simply have to click on the analytics icon available in each post, as shown in the image below.

For more information, see our article on how to use Twitter. As for the most important metrics provided by this Social Network, are the following:

- ➢ Retweets: indicates how many times people have shared your publication.
- ➢ Favorites: indicates the number of times people have marked your tweet as a favorite.
- ➢ Answers: Shows how many replies your posts have obtained.

Statistics on LinkedIn

In terms of Social Network statistics, LinkedIn's metrics are among the most relevant, since it is a Social Network fully dedicated to the world of work and business. Thus, to know the performance data of your individual accounts, you only have to consult the option "Who has seen your profile" in the tab "Profile" inside the site.

The main metrics that LinkedIn offers you in your individual profile are:

➢ Profile Views: Shows the number of times people have visited your profile in the last 90 days.

➢ Actions Performed: indicates the number of times you have generated interactions (comments, recommendations or Likes and times you have added new contacts).

➢ Details of who visited your profile: indicate how many people with detailed jobs have visited your profile.

Also, in LinkedIn you can see the *statistics* of your Business Pages. To get to know them, simply go to your Page and click on the "Analysis" tab.

After logging in, you'll find each of the posts you've shared and their corresponding statistics.

The metrics that LinkedIn offers you for each post of your business page are:

> - Impressions: shows the number of times your post has been viewed.
> - Clicks: indicates the number of times users have clicked on your company's content, name, or logo.
> - Interactions: displays how many comments, recommendations and times your post has been shared.
> - Participation: shows the number of interactions added to the number of clicks, divided by the number of impressions received by the post.

Statistics in Google+

Other social network statistics that cannot be missing from this list are those offered by Google+. To access the analytics of your Google+ page, go to the menu on the left of your page and click on 'My Business'. Then you will see a welcome announcement appear and finally you will access the statistics panel shown below.

As you may have noticed, in the same panel you can obtain metrics from your Google+ Page, from your YouTube channel (if you have one) and from Google

Analytics, in case you have an account in that service. In order to know in detail, the statistics of your Google+ page, you have to press the "View Statistics" button located to the right of the first box displayed in the previous image, titled "Statistics". Then you can view the metrics of your Google+ Page in much more detail.

The metrics that Google+ offers you with respect to your page are the following:

➢ Visibility: shows the total number of visits to your page. By clicking on the drop-down arrow next to the title "4,766 visits in total", you will be able to see the detail of the views of your profile, your photos and your publications.

➢ Engagement: displays the indicators "Action of publications" (clicks, +1 received, comments and times your post has been shared), "Recent publications" (displays your last 5 updates) and "Average actions by type of publication" (shows the interactions, +1 and comments of your links, photos, texts and videos). To see this data, you must press the "Commitment" button next to the "Visibility" button shown in the image above.

➢ Audience: This parameter shows your new followers and gives you data about your audience, which you can filter by country, age and sex. This feature is enabled only when your Google+ page has more than 200 followers.

Statistics in Pinterest

In the case of Pinterest, only people with business accounts can access the statistics. In order to know them, you have to enter to the configuration menu inside your profile, and then you have to select the option "Analytics".

Next you will see the General Statistics panel, in which you will get a panel of your account situation in the form of graphs, as you can see in the image below. You will also be able to establish which period of time you wish to analyze, in order to know the peaks of success or inactivity in relation to your publications.

The most important panels for analyzing your Pinterest account are the following:

> ➢ Your Pinterest profile: here you will find the number of times your profile has been visited and how many clicks your links to your site have received, among other data.
> ➢ Your Most Viewed Pins: Shows you the number of interactions your pins received, as shown in the image below. There you can see the number of impressions, repines, clicks and I Like that has received each of your posts.
> ➢ Your Audience: This is another important panel of Pinterest Analytics, as it shows you data about your audience that allows you to know it better,

to guide your strategy and choose your content with greater effectiveness. Some of the data you will find are the age, sex, interests and origin of your audience.

As you may have noticed, *social network statistics are becoming* increasingly relevant in terms of digital marketing, which is why I advise you to check your account metrics frequently. This will allow you to measure your efforts at Social Media and know how close you are to meeting your goals.

SOCIAL NETWORK STATISTICS 2019: USERS OF FACEBOOK, TWITTER, INSTAGRAM, YOUTUBE, LINKEDIN, WHATSAPP AND OTHERS

Active Facebook users

In January 2019 Facebook had about 2,271 million active users in a month.

When Facebook is used properly in the Social Media Marketing strategy, it is possible to generate a significant traffic of valuable audience for the brand to the website, which is where we sell.

Growths like this, forces us responsible for social networks in companies to include it in the Social Media Marketing strategies of all companies regardless of their size, category and audience.

According to the WeAreSocial and Hootsuite study, 43% of the potential reach of Facebook ads are women and 57% are men. 35% of the audience is under 25 years of age and more than 90% access through mobile devices. This makes it important that all links from this social network to the website or online store should have good browsing experience on these types of devices.

When viewing Facebook as a business channel it is critical to know the potential reach of ads by age range. In percentages the distribution would be like this:

> In reviewing the ranking of the 20 countries with the largest Facebook audience, we identified several Latin American countries: Brazil, Mexico, Argentina and Colombia. In users the distribution would be like this:

Active users of Instagram

Instagram has more than 1,000 million active users in a month.

This is the social network with greater growth, has managed to double the number of users in just two years.

Unlike Facebook, Instagram does not allow you to generate traffic to the website with publications on your timeline, however it should be included in the Social Network Marketing strategy due to its significant growth and because it allows you to bring your brand closer to its audience.

The age and gender range of the potential audience of Instagram advertising is identified. It shows how the 1,000 million users are distributed in the different age ranges, it is important to note that the range between 18 and 24 years is very important in this social network.

It is surprising to find that there are 4 countries in Latin America (Brazil, Mexico, Argentina and Colombia) in the list of 19 countries with the largest number of users in the world. In number of users the distribution is as follows:

Active Twitter users

Twitter has more than 326 million active users in a month.

This social network is one of the slowest growing, however it becomes indispensable for the social media marketing strategy due to several aspects:

➢ Your strength in real-time information.
➢ It can become the official means of communication for brands.
➢ It is a social network that is mostly public what allows brands to make social listening through it.

Twitter users by age range differs significantly with Facebook and Instagram highlighting the important access of people in the range of 35 to 49 years.

Active LinkedIn Users

LinkedIn has 303 million active users in one month and more than 500 million registered users.

This social network aimed at professional groups also had a significant growth in recent years and has evolved in recent years from being a channel of social media recruitment to one where they share value-added information from different professions.

LinkedIn is another social media channel necessary for all companies that want to use social networks as a channel of communication and marketing.

The most important age range for this social network is 25 to 34 years and a strong presence in the range 35 to 54 years.

> It is important to highlight that there are 4 countries in Latin America (Brazil, Mexico, Argentina and Colombia) among the 20 countries with the most LinkedIn users in the world.

Active Snapchat users

Snapchat has more than 287 million active users in a month.

This social network aimed primarily at young people has slowed its growth since Instagram launched its Instagram Stories service.

Snapchat is a very important social network for businesses when their primary audience is teenagers.

As for the 20 countries with the most Snapchat users, only Mexico and Brazil appear.

8. Active users of Pinterest

Pinterest has more than 250 million active users in a month.

This is another social network that has not had significant growth in recent years, however, I consider it very useful in the social media marketing strategy.

Active YouTube users

YouTube has more than 1.9 billion active users in a month.

Although YouTube has excellent social functionalities, brands use it as a video repository since the videos that become vital do so through other social networks.

Active users of WhatsApp

WhatsApp has more than 1.5 billion active users in a month.

Although this is not considered a social network, it is a very important communication channel for companies.

As WhatsApp is a very personal means of communication, it should only be used for the operation of the business and not to execute commercial and marketing strategies.

Detailed report of user's social networks (WeAreSocial and Hootsuite)

Facebook reaches 2,000 million users

> Facebook reached the symbolic figure of 2,000 million active monthly users, announced the social network.
>
> "Now there are two billion people connecting and building communities on Facebook every month," the group's vice president, Naomi Gleit, announced in an online post.
>
> "This is made possible by the millions of communities and individuals who share and create important contributions on Facebook," the social network added.
>
> According to the group, there are more than 1 billion people who use "groups," and more than 800 million who give "like" to something on Facebook every day.
>
> "We're moving forward to connect the whole world, and now, we've made the world closer," said co-founder and group leader Mark Zuckerberg on his own Facebook page.
>
> "It's an honor to make this trip with you," he added.

Created in 2004, Facebook has become an internet giant.

In the first quarter of 2017 recorded a net profit of $3,060 million dollars, an increase of 76.3% in one year, with a turnover of $8,003 million dollars, an increase of 49.2 percent.

As of March 31, the company had about 1.94 billion internet users using its service per month, a 17% increase from the previous year.

Facebook is looking to expand its huge user base, especially in developing countries where the social network currently has lower penetration rates.

Instagram statistics that you should know

You should know that Instagram is not only the social network in which photos are shared with filters. It's almost one billion active monthly users -according to the latest statistics- are not only looking for beautiful images. Here they build marketing strategies and brands (many brands) that develop interesting visual and business aesthetics. Instagram users grow 5% per quarter

Instagram offers up to 58 times more interaction per follower than Facebook and 150 times more than Twitter, according to a survey conducted by Forrestser Research, a U.S. market research company.

While in Latin America, Mexico is the country with the most registered users in the region: 16 million, followed by Argentina with 11 million.

In this book we share statistics that will be useful when thinking about your marketing strategy in Instagram:

70% of the hashtags in Instagram have been created by brands.

We insist on the use of hashtags in Instagram because they allow brands to gain exposure in very segmented audiences or with specific areas of interest. By generating their own hashtags, brands organize the conversations that occur around them.

Hashtags containing between 21 and 24 characters perform better than shorter ones because they are more specific and attractive for connecting with your audience.

And how many hashtags are too much or too little? Although Instagram allows you to use up to 30 hashtags, we do not recommend this figure. A good number is about 11 and if you have doubts about which strategy to follow, here are some tips:

➢ It combines hashtags of 4 categories: the very popular (from 100,000 to 500,000 associated publications), the moderately popular (between 10,000 and 100,000 associated publications) and the specific (10,000 associated publications).
➢ That your hashtags are focused on a business and topics that your target audience.
➢ Use hashtags exclusive to your brand or associated with any launch or campaign.

#WeekVoluntariadoBBVA is a campaign carried out by BBVA so that its collaborators can integrate with the brand and experience the solidarity mission that the financial institution has. So far, the hashtag is associated with 44 publications.

If you need advice to monitor keywords or the hashtags and locations of Instagram, in Sprout Social we have the tools for it.

15 million Latin American companies have a profile in Instagram.

And we have nearly 2 million active advertisers in this region. Of these, the most commonly used strategy is the use of live stories and videos to connect with your audience.

An interesting example is what Sprite Mexico (@spritemx) did: it relied on stories to inspire young people by conveying the message that Sprite can overcome any difficulty. For this campaign they used the hashtag #BornToRefresh.

According to brand data, thanks to this campaign 18 points were increased in the memory of the ad, 4 in the consideration of the brand as first choice and 2 in valuation.

"Thanks to Instagram Stories we can reach our young audience using content tailored to their interests that grabs attention in seconds and conveys the message of our campaign. Karen Arreola, Director of Sprite Mexico's Smart Management Center

80% of Instagram users follow at least one company

According to data from the Facebook summit in Brazil (2017), 80% of people with an Instagram account follow a company, while 59% have used this network to discover a brand or buy a product. Vishal Shah, Instagram's business product manager, stressed that brands should take advantage of this opportunity to grow their business.

Johnson & Johnson used the visual potential of Instagram's stories to unlock the secrets of influential women in Latin America as part of Carefree's positioning campaign (@carefreearg).

Using the hashtag #vossabés the campaign, according to company figures, achieved an increase of 17 points in the memory of the ad and 6 points in the consideration of the brand.

One out of four advertisements on Instagram are videos

Vertical videos are the big trend in Instagram. We can see it in live broadcasts, stories and on Instagram TV. This trend will continue throughout next year and this format is already available on YouTube and Vimeo.

According to Kevin Systrom, co-founder of Instagram, video views on the platform increased by 150% over the past 6 months. It also increased the average length of branded video ads by more than 60%.

It is estimated that more than 2 million advertisers use different types of Instagram video ads. Among the advantages of this type of vertical videos is that they show the image much more centered and avoids cutting heads or faces.

Please note that these ads can last between 3 and 60 seconds, include a call to action and up to 2,200 characters. You can also opt for carousel ads that allow you to include up to 5 videos in a single ad.

For the launch of a new product, L'Oréal in Argentina prepared a campaign with video advertisements in Instagram Stories aimed at women between 18 and 54 years old. L'Oréal used carousel ads showing in sequences how to get healthy hair. According to brand data, they managed to increase the memory of the ad by 14.7 points, the intention to buy by 3.3 points, and the memory of the message by 4.8 points.

Coca-Cola Mexico also developed an Instagram campaign with carousel video ads. The aim was for users to share everyday situations divided into 3 sequences: a meal, a meal accompanied by this brand and sharing this drink with friends.

The campaign included emojis and calls to action. These videos reached 14 million users on Instagram and achieved one million video views.

The brands in Instagram have 58 times more participation than in other social networks

Instagram is consecrated as one of the most powerful platforms for business. The brands with the best strategies report a participation rate per follower of 4.21%, 58 times more than on Facebook and 120 times more than on Twitter.

An Instagram Business profile allows you to add additional contact information that is not available for personal profiles. This information includes a business telephone number and an address.

Publications tagged with another user or location have significantly higher participation rates. It is therefore important for brands to add "with whom" and "where" in their Instagram publications.

"90% of Instagram users are under 35." Source ScienceDaily.

A third of the stories most seen in Instagram belong to brands

According to Instagram data, the brands are making good use of the stories. In just one month, more than 50% of the companies in this network published stories.

"The marks are rising to Instagram Stories with more than twice the frequency of Snapchat." Source Adweek.

And why are we interested in these data? Because from these numbers we see results in the users. At least 75% of these take some action after seeing advertisements on Instagram, such as visiting a website or making a purchase. A survey conducted by the Global web index found that more than a third of Instagram users have purchased a product from their mobile device.

But it is not enough just to publish commercial content, it is also necessary to analyze how these ads behave and thus know which publications like and which meet the expectations of our followers and allows us to know them better.

Sprout Social offers services that help you understand the performance of your campaigns on Instagram (and other social networks).

Let's look at the case of Burger King in Spain and its veto of onions during International Kissing Day. The brand used Instagram Stories to promote its Onion Blackout campaign and to inform its audience that no onion would be sold on Kiss Day.

They introduced a couple who avoided each other when they sold onions in this food chain and kissed each other when the brand stopped selling this product. Instagram Stories was used allowing the audience to click to advance the video and know what was going on when the onion was sold or not.

The company got 60% more shares from its users, three times more attention and twice as many full plays of this type of video (sequence format) than with single-video ads.

92% of Instagram users consider user-generated content to be more reliable than commercial content.

According to studies, 86% of businesses have employed CGU, but only 27% have done so following a strategy. A first step may be to create an exclusive branded hashtag for our business or campaign.

Many brands are taking advantage of CGU. This is the case with Birchbox, an online make-up and beauty subscription service that tries to reach its audience through contests that we learn about by following the brand's Instagram, sharing its hashtags and tagging friends on Instagram. It has been proven that this strategy makes the number of followers grow rapidly and is a way to achieve organic growth.

By employing CGU, brands give users the opportunity to tell real stories. Not in vain, according to the research company Ipsos, the millennials claim that they trust 50% more in the CGU than in any other type of content.

Burger King Spain invites its followers to share content related to its brand using the following message: "Label us in your most beautiful photos with our products, and you can win a free Whopper menu if your photo is selected as the image of the week!

The Argentine brand of diaries and notebooks Monoblock works with CGU through the experience of drawing. In the image appears the illustrator Pepita Sandwich and the legend that accompanies and portrays the experience of the artist when she draws. The brand invites its users to tell how they feel.

It is estimated that by 2019 there will be 32 million sponsored publications in Instagram.

If there is a preferred platform for influencers to share sponsored content is Instagram. In 2016 alone, there were almost 9 million such publications and predictions predict quadrupling this figure for this year.

If you Google the term "Latin Influencers", you will find half a million results and these numbers are reflected in the millions of dollars they move. In 2017 alone,

Influencer Marketing has moved close to 4 billion dollars. Here are some of the most popular:

Lele Pons is a Venezuelan American YouTube star and one of the most influential Latinas. Time magazine named her as one of the most influential people on the Internet and her videos have more than 1.3 billion hits.

Peruvian actress Alessandra Denegri is a fashion icon. Your Instagram account has 175,000 followers. Many brands in the beauty and fashion industry choose her as their spokesperson.

Dulce Candy is a Mexican American youtuber and one of the main Latin influences. It has more than two million YouTube subscribers and 1.1 million Instagram followers. She works with brands like Pixi and Dr. Jart.

Active monthly users of Instagram

In June 2018, Instagram reached 1,000 million active monthly users (Statista, 2018) - a great achievement for Instagram! More than 500 million active users use the platform daily. From there, the Instagram application is one of the most popular social networks in the world. A little over 5 years ago, in June 2013, Instagram had only 130 million active monthly users. Since then, it has grown 10 times.

Instagram is a social network that allows users to share and edit photos and videos. Outside of social networks, only Facebook and YouTube have more active users daily than Instagram. At one point it was mainly used by teenagers and young millennials, but now Instagram continues to grow as one of the most popular social networking platforms, and the data tells us that it will not change in the short term.

So, if you were still wondering if your brand should spend time and money to invest in Instagram, the huge amount of active monthly users should be an affirmative indication. Our team recently wrote a beginner's guide to selling on Instagram to help you understand the many nuances of the platform.

The Power of Instagram

With one billion active users per month, we are not surprised that Instagram is the second most interactive social network (Emarketer, 2018). In first place is secured by Facebook. This statistic shows that more than 60.6% of internet users in the United States access Facebook at least once a month. And when it comes to Instagram, 37.4% of Internet users will access this social networking platform at least once a month this year. That's an amazing percentage!

People have been wondering how they can increase their followers on Instagram and improve their level of interaction with this audience. If you've been neglecting your company's Instagram account, now is probably the right time to build community and improve your interaction on this social network.

Young adults love Instagram

71% of the one billion active monthly users in the Instagram application are less than 35 years old (Statista, 2019). This statistic provides information on the distribution of Instagram users worldwide as of January 2019. The most popular age range is for users between the ages of 25 and 34, followed by users between the ages of 18 and 24. Does your target audience include this demographic group?

Understanding social network demographics will help you determine which platforms make the most sense for your brand. This way, you'll ensure that you don't waste time creating content for a platform where your audience doesn't have a presence. If your target market is young adults, you know that Instagram is the right place for you. Once you know this, you can start producing the right type of Instagram content that suits the needs of your users and use the right phrases for this social network.

Average time spent in Instagram

People spend almost as much time on Instagram as they do on Facebook. The amount of time that Android users spend on Instagram is close to that of Facebook. In June 2018, Facebook users spent an average of 58 minutes per day on the platform, compared to 57 minutes per day for Instagram users.

Time spent on Instagram is important because the more time people spend on the application, the more ads they see and the more opportunities they have to get to know your brand. Instagram also revealed that the introduction of the Instagram stories increased the amount of time people spent on the application every day. But not only the time spent on Instagram matters, but also the time of day when users are most active on the platform. In this way, you will know the best times to publish in Instagram for your brand.

Companies are using Instagram

With the growing popularity of Instagram, approximately 71% of U.S. companies claim to use Instagram for their business (Mention, 2018). The same study also reveals that 7 out of 10 hashtags in Instagram are branded. And more than 80% of companies consider Instagram interactions to be the most important metric. Interaction in Instagram can be one of the most important KPIs for many marketers, but measuring it is not an easy task. With the Instagram platform evolving rapidly, it is difficult to keep up with updates and what to measure.

Companies have a great opportunity to promote their products through Instagram. Not only is there a large market, but there is an interested audience that you can reach without spending large sums of money. If you are looking for suggestions and ideas on how to advertise on Instagram for your brand.

The impact of Instagram for brands

83% of Instagram users say they discover new products and services on Instagram (Facebook, 2019). This means that they are using Instagram as a channel for inspiration. The same study also reveals that by being on Instagram, brands can make a positive impression on potential buyers.

Instagram is not only playing a role as a discovery engine for brands, but is now further reducing the gap between buyers and sellers by presenting options such as Instagram purchase and the new Instagram checkout. The potential impact of using Instagram for vendors is growing. Instagram may play a role in every part of your customer's purchasing process. Buyers are looking for inspiration through Instagram or researching products before making a purchase decision. It is in these steps along the way that marketers can influence buyers who use the Instagram platform.

Using Instagram Stories

In August 2016, Instagram launched the stories of Instagram. This feature allows users to take photos or videos that disappear after 24 hours. After launching this feature, people started sharing much more on Instagram. 500 million Instagram accounts use Instagram Stories every day (Instagram, 2018). Not only that, but 1/3 of the most viewed GI stories are from companies.

Before the Instagram stories, people only shared most of their important moments, which used not to be daily. Instagram hit the nail on the head with the stories, giving people a good reason to share their everyday moments without having to keep the content in their profile. This is also a great opportunity for companies to increase their visibility. There is an article that shows how you can create Instagram stories to increase your audience.

Instagram users follow the brands

50% of Instagram users follow at least one brand (Mention, 2018), which means that companies have a great opportunity to increase their reach through this social network. Whether you have a local brand or a company worldwide, you have the potential to improve your visibility by using it.

With an Instagram Business profile, brands can add their additional contact information, which is not an option available for personal profiles. This includes a company phone number and address. If you have an Instagram Business profile, you also have access to Instagram analysis which can provide you with data on impressions and scopes per publication, as well as more information on your demographic profile. This can help you understand what kind of content your audience likes best. So, whether it's food, clothing or any niche you're interested in, you can be sure there will be users interested in following you or your brand on Instagram.

The level of interaction in Instagram does matter

The engagement or level of interaction in Instagram is increasing for brands. It increased by 29% between October 2017 and May 2018 (Socialbakers, 2018). This means that brands generate 4 times more interactions in Instagram compared to Facebook.

While we understand that the level of Instagram interaction is important for brands, the question remains, what is Instagram interaction and how is it measured? The interaction of Instagram is the degree of participation that your followers show towards your content. This could be in the form of likes, comments or actions. Instagram is a platform based on visual content, which is one of the reasons why it has such a high level of interaction. It offers a platform for different types of content creation, such as photos, videos, live videos, stories and also the IGTV application. This increases the creativity of the content by giving you a wide variety of content types to choose from. If you are a brand or a business, you should take advantage of Instagram's potential to improve interactions. We have many tips for you to improve your levels of interaction there.

Instagram has an impact on the buyer's purchasing path

We have already analyzed the impact of Instagram for brands, but now we are going to take it one step further. Instagram helps 80% of Instagram users decide whether to buy a product or service (Facebook, 2019). Instagram users report that they made a purchase decision based on something they saw while browsing the application. Therefore, if your brand does not include Instagram in its social network marketing strategy, you are missing a great opportunity. Especially if your business is aimed at millennials.

There are several different tactics you can use to impact a buyer's decision on Instagram. So, whether you use ads, make creative stories or include the most relevant hashtags, everything can matter if you do it right.

Conclusion

Over the years, Instagram has proven to be a powerful marketing tool for companies looking to expand both their visibility and reach. We hope these Instagram statistics for 2019 have helped you understand why your brand should invest in Instagram and already have more ideas about what to do on the platform.

Summary: Instagram Statistics

Here is a summary of Instagram statistics for 2019:

1. There are one billion active monthly users in Instagram.
2. Instagram is the network with the highest levels of interaction after Facebook.
3. 71% of the one billion active monthly users in the Instagram application are under 35 years old.
4. Instagram users spend an average of 53 minutes per day on the app.
5. 500 million IG accounts use Instagram histories every day.
6. 83% of Instagram users discover new products and services there.
7. Instagram can generate 4 times more interactions compared to Facebook.
8. 71% of U.S. companies use Instagram.
9. Instagram helps 80% of its users to decide to buy a product or service.

10. 50% of Instagrammers follow at least one business.

Social Media Marketing 2019-2020: Volume 2

How to Build Your Personal Brand to Become an Influencer by Leveraging Facebook, Twitter, YouTube & Instagram

By

Income Mastery

INTRODUCTION

Did you know that social networks have become the main marketing medium in the world? Wouldn't you like to manage your personal brand directly and without as much complication as you would in a traditional television channel or paid advertising?

Marketing has always been a fundamental tool when it comes to business. For some years these studies have been deepened even more, having clear patterns that shape and govern marketing in order to improve this tool. In the current era we find digital marketing and social networks, which helps us to promote a product or service that we want to direct to a specific audience. With this tool we can have a better exposure on our sales between companies, and our products will be launched to a large number of people who are potential buyers who can generate higher revenues in a staggered manner, this would leave a higher return, which is the purpose of any company or brand for profit. The marketing in social networks has the great advantage that the exhibition of everything that we want to sell to the public is given free, this is understood since social networks have zero cost at the time of being used. Every company aims to have a high utility, and this makes the savings of advertising in media such as television, radio or panels is very high, because their costs include payment of personnel, structure, maintenance of equipment, among others, which increases costs.

Influencers are not just people who have a channel on social networks like YouTube, Facebook or Twitter, because influencing goes far beyond this simple terminology. In order to be an influencer, you must have creative ideas, and specially a channel on different platforms that have a better reach to the general public. It should also have totally original themes and content, and video editions and general publications that are interactive and of interest to your audience. No detail is of minor importance. For example, if we start with content, what did you publish? If it's a kitchen channel or a travel and adventure channel, we can't expose the same theme or prototype.

It is also important to know the age and preferences of the audience we are going to target, for example, if we are going to target an audience over 30 years, we must have much more serious content and editions, place faint colors, less scandalous, while if we are dedicated to generate content for a young audience, for example, in the age of 15 to 25 years, we have to be very interactive, use bright colors, fast language and videos edited with changing images that generate a visual impact. Doing previous studies is very important. For example, we can use web surveys to find out the ages and tastes of our audience, so we can be much closer and know what to produce, how to produce and when to do it.

After making it clear what topics you are going to perform and what audience you are going to focus on, it is important to have a name or nickname with which our audience will identify us, that nickname should be remarkable, easy to pronounce, totally unique and should attract attention as this will identify us to the audience forever. With this name we are going to be called, our real name will disappear, and it will be with this nick as all the people will know and identify us.

It is important to know how to choose, in which social network platform we are going to place our content, among the most used we have YouTube, Facebook, Instagram and Twitter, each one fulfills its function in a different way and offers innovative tools that help in the development that has the influence. From this you can find that they all have different functions, for example, YouTube has as a feature to be a website that shows only videos and groups them through the pages or channels created by users, these accounts where you can upload videos are called channels, have certain regulatory laws under which all influencers are governed.

Facebook, on the other hand, is an application that is also developed on cell phones and on a web page that has a greater arrival where pages are created. These pages have a name and can also create video publications, photos, files in general, also subject to internal rules proposed by Facebook to protect minors. This platform blocks violence and adult content, and if the site insists on using this content it is temporarily blocked, or in the worst case, removed.

Instagram is a platform associated with Facebook, now owned by the same owner, also presents a very massive arrival in terms of number of users who use it. The added value of this platform is that you can make publications called stories that can be fixed or can also be momentary with a duration of 24 hours, in these stories you can make surveys, upload videos with photographic effects also with filters own application that is the unique seal of this platform.

On the other hand, Twitter presents totally different characteristics, immediacy is its strength as publications have to be very concentrated content, it does not have the freedom to make extensive publications. The use of hashtags generates global trends, it is also an added value in itself that has no publishing filters as it is an open social network for users to publish what they want.

In conclusion, these platforms have become the new communication channels of the new era, with an attraction that traditional media have not yet developed: immediacy in direct communications with users or consumers of the profile.

YouTube

The YouTube platform is a company created on February 14, 2005 owned by Google. It is a video hosting service available to the entire public, functioning as a means of mass communication and dissemination. Its main web portal (Youtube.com) offers all kinds of video clips such as movies (in any language), television programs or their summary, viral and fun videos for the masses, music clips with the current trends, plus video blogs and YouTube Gaming. It is important to point out that YouTube as a platform has a series of regulations on its content, where it indicates that all its material is copyrighted, either by its creator or by YouTube, thus respecting the copyright of each material.

YouTube was founded in February 2005 by three former PayPal employees at the time, Chad Hurley, Steve Chen and Jawed Karim, and in October 2006 was purchased by Google Inc. for 1.65 billion dollars. The idea of this platform was born due to the difficulties they experienced trying to share videos recorded during a party in San Francisco, however, the main idea of the development of the project was to create a dating page, where people could rate themselves based on their videos. It is currently the most used website of its kind, as it became a direct reference for Internet users to locate any audiovisual material. As an important fact, we must point out that links to videos on this platform can be inserted into blogs, websites, emails and social networks (Twitter, Facebook, LinkedIn and the like) using a certain HTML code.

The web domain was made public on February 15, 2005, and the following month, by April 23, the first YouTube video entitled Me at the Zoo was uploaded. At the moment this video still exists, but it has only reached a little more than 51 million visits. In its first months of launch, its founders see that users had diverted the original idea of the project, as they uploaded any type of videos, but the surprising thing is that traffic skyrocketed when people started placing video links on YouTube to their MySpace profiles.

By the end of 2005, YouTube was visited at least 250 million times a day, and by May 2006 it reached its 2,000 million views per day, but 3 months later it reached the average of 7,000 million views per day, making it the tenth most visited portal in the United States. By now, and according to the New York Post, YouTube could have cost at least $1 billion.

To compete with this, MySpace.com and Google decide to launch their own versions of YouTube, without succeeding.

Steps to use YouTube

The YouTube platform allows you to watch videos, create videos, and even create your own YouTube channel. If you want this, you must follow the steps below:

To view videos

1. **Sign in with your Google Account (Gmail)**. When you sign in you get many benefits including the ability to comment, save videos for later viewing, subscribe to channels, and upload your own media. Create a free Google Account if you want access to all YouTube features. Remember that YouTube accounts are now linked to Google accounts in general.

2. **Use the search bar to find videos.** The YouTube search bar works in the same way as the Google search bar and shows you predictive results as you search. When searching for a video, you can usually only enter related terms if you don't know the title, so many related searches will show videos tagged with good descriptions. You can also use the search filters to perform more specific searches.

3. **Explore YouTube channels**. If you don't know exactly what you're looking for, you can explore

the most popular content on YouTube by reviewing the different categories that appear on the main screen. Click the "Browse Channels" button in the left navigation menu. Channels are sorted by category so you can quickly watch the most popular channels according to your favorite interests. Remember that a YouTube channel is a page created by a person, group or company. These channels store all the content uploaded by the channel owner and function as a profile page for all YouTube users who follow it, or recommendations for those who don't follow it.

4. **Subscribe to your favorite channels**. The channels you subscribe to will alert you each time a new video is uploaded to those profiles. To subscribe to a channel, click on the red "Subscribe" button located below the video for that channel (the one you were watching) or click on the "Subscribe" button on the official channel page or profile.

5. **Leave comments**. If you are logged in, you can leave your comments on the videos that have the comments option enabled, if you are not logged in, you can only read the comments. To leave a comment, click on the "Share what you think" field below the video, and write your comment. You can also reply to other comments by clicking

on the "Reply" link below the comment. Not all videos have the comment option enabled.

6. **Add a video to your "Watch Later" list**. If in your navigation within the YouTube platform you find a video that you liked and want to see later, you can add it to your "View Later" list so that you can quickly access it at any time. Under the name of the video, click on the "+ Add to" button and select your "View Later" list or another playlist you have created.

If on the contrary, you want to upload videos, you have the following options.

1. **Edit the video before uploading it.** YouTube has some video editing tools, but it's best to edit it yourself before uploading. You can use a video editing program to combine all the videos you want to make into one. It's perfect for editing multiple shots together or compiling multiple videos. Videos should be less than 15 minutes long until you verify your account. Tell YouTube your cell phone number so you can verify your account. YouTube will send you a code which you must enter to verify your account.

2. **Upload the video**. When you upload a video, it will be added to your personal channel. You don't have to configure anything in your channel

in order to upload the video. Later, if you do this more regularly, you'll be able to customize your channel and build a subscriber network. You can also record directly from your webcam, skipping the video upload process. Once you're done you can use YouTube's video editor to make minor changes to the video.

3. **Add a title and description**. A good title and a good description can make a big difference in getting views. It's best if the title and description are relevant to the content of the video, otherwise you probably won't get many views. The description can be read under the video when someone watches it. The description is used to put more details about the aspects of the video, link your video to related pages or explain something else you want about the video.

4. **Add tags**. Tags complement your video to appear in search results as a related video. Labels are single words or short phrases that function as small descriptions. Using good tags can significantly increase the views or visits your video gets. Don't exaggerate with too many tags or misleading tags, otherwise YouTube's search function will penalize you, preventing the visitors from getting any.

5. **Adjust your video's privacy settings**. When you upload a video, you have three basic privacy options. You can configure it so that anyone can search for the video, so that it is only seen by entering the URL or so that the video is private and so only the users you allow can see it. If you're setting a video to 'Private' and want to share it with specific people, they'll need to have a Google Account (Gmail).

6. **Monetize your video.** If you comply with the requirements that YouTube establishes, you can earn money with the advertising views that are in your video. If you don't get a lot of visits, you probably don't make a lot of money, or you don't make anything, however, the big influencers on YouTube make millions of dollars and euros a year.

7. **Share your video.** Publish your videos on your favorite social network (Twitter, Facebook, LinkedIn, etc.) or insert the video in your blog. It's important that you share your video so that it becomes viral, because the more people you share it with, the more they will be able to share it if they like the content. YouTube has built-in video sharing features on most major social networks. If you want to insert the video on your

website, YouTube will provide you with the code you will need to do so.

Now, the time has come to explain the main definition to comply with the above mentioned: Create A YouTube Channel. Here are the steps to do it:

1. **Conceptualizes the channel(s)**. The channels are part of your YouTube user page. Each YouTube account comes with a channel and you can create additional channels in your account. Each channel comes with an associated Google+ page, which will allow you to cross-promote.

2. **I design the channel with the personality you want to give it**. The design is the poster at the top of your channel that will allow you to distinguish it from others and solidify your brand. This design must be related to the content of your videos or your personality, because it will be your letter of introduction to the public.

3. **Defines the name and description of the channel**. A good and correct description will help you attract people to your channel, and a good name will help users remember it. Your description should include links to your website, as well as a brief description of the

purpose of your channel. If you change the channel name, the account name associated with Google+ will also change.

4. **Develop and debug your content**. By having your channel set up, you must start uploading content and attracting visitors. Create and publish quality content on a regular basis so you can build a loyal fan base. Become a YouTube partner for more exposure and access to advanced authoring tools.

YouTube and partners

YouTube has launched some associated services to complement the experience of users on the network, which are:

a. **YouTube For Kids**: This is the children's version of YouTube, which has restricted content so that it is only used to search for children's content neatly. In addition, it has a sound limiter or timer to take care of the time when children are exposed to the screens and do not harm them. This is a perfect application for parents, as it gives them an assurance that their children will not surf or see inappropriate content for their age.

b. **YouTube Gaming**: This is a YouTube service and application dedicated to gamers, which was born to compete with Twitch TV. YouTube Gaming became one of the favorite video playback services by gamers. In this service you will find a more comfortable interface for the gamer public, as there is even a chat where viewers can interact with another player, in addition, from this platform you can upload games from Android to Google Play Games, so that other users can see your record in the games.

c. **YouTube NewsWire**: Is a channel created in collaboration with StoryFul with the goal of presenting world news to this platform. So far, it's just a channel.

d. **YouTube Music**: Seeks to compete with Spotify and Deezer. This application seeks to make it easier for YouTube users to play their favorite songs without the need for video. Its interface is designed to make it easy for the user to locate their favorite artists, in addition to presenting only the musical themes of the platform.

e. **YouTube Red**: It started as YouTube Music Key, which was intended to be a premium version of the platform, but then progressed to become YouTube Red, which is the same premium service as YouTube. Its price is 10 dollars a month, and you have the following services: offline reproduction, without ads and in the background, access to exclusive content created specifically for subscribers.

Evolution and improvements in video quality.

With almost 14 years in the market, YouTube has not been left behind in the vanguard of video quality. Many users of the Google Video network (at the beginning of the platform) and other video sites complained about the quality of it, as they say that some videos are pixelated, since most of the time it is due to the balance between image quality and data transmission speed on the network, or audio and video are not synchronized. At the time, videos should not occupy more than 2GB on the disk space and were allowed a duration of less than 16 minutes, which means up to 15 minutes with 59 seconds. All the videos uploaded to the network were converted to 320x240 and 480x360 pixels at 30 frames per second. However, most videos hosted on the web before March 2008 are available in lower resolution.

At the end of 2008 we began to incorporate videos with HD format with 720p quality, and for 2009 its quality rose to 1080p, allowing you to choose the desired quality depending on the speed of the Internet that is available for the time when the clip is being viewed, because, if we have a low Internet speed, it will be more difficult to load the video causing it to stop all the time while you try to watch. For this, you must go to the bottom right corner of the video and press the button as a gear, where you can choose the desired video format.

By November 25, 2008, the YouTube platform changes the aspect ratio of his video player from standard (4:3) to cinema format (16:9), joining the standard for LCD and Plasma TVs, as well as joining the company's futuristic vision of streaming full-length movies in the future. This change of appearance was made with all the clips that YouTube has on its platform, and the videos that were in standard format (4:3) appear with black stripes on the sides to fill the space they leave for the cinema format (16:9).

A few years later QHD (1440p) and 4K or Ultra HD (Ultra High Definition) resolutions were added, but by July 2015 the 8K format (7.680x4.320 pixels) was added, being up to 16 times higher than High Definition (HD). The following year, specifically in November 2016, the support for uploading and playing videos in HDR was integrated.

Its updates were not only for the reproduction of videos, but also for the reproduction of videogames for gamers, because in June 2014 YouTube introduced the videos with reproduction of 60 frames per second, something comparable with the resolution of the graphics cards of

High range. These videos are reproduced with a resolution of 720p or higher. The quality of clips uploaded to YouTube are standard quality (SQ), high quality (HQ) and high definition (HD), which are currently expressed in resolution numbers.

By January 2015, the company Google announces that YouTube will allow to upload videos in 360°, something completely revolutionary. However, since March 13, 2015, 360° videos can be viewed from Google Cardboard, a virtual reality platform. YouTube 360° is available for all virtual reality platforms.

Restrictions on copying and copyright of clips on the platform

Material posted on the YouTube platform is protected against copying and copyright infringement by its creators. In fact, since its creation, videos uploaded to YouTube were played in flash format (FLV), belonging to Adobe Flash, which prevents and prevents users from making digital copies easily, however, many programmers have developed over time many tools that allow, without authorization or permission from YouTube, the download of clips hosted on the website. There are currently many applications for downloading this material without permission from YouTube, also in High Definition (HD). To prevent this, the Google Chrome browser applies a restriction so that Chrome Web Store extensions cannot download videos.

In the terms of copyright protection, YouTube allows videos published with music or videos copyrighted within another video, even if this is an infringement, however, only make restrictions and penalties to persons who infringe after a third call of attention after a complaint of copyright infringement, causing the suspension of the video and the account for a time determined by YouTube.

According to YouTube, by 2017 **the sanctions** were as follows:

- In the event that a current or archived live stream is removed for copyright infringement, access to the live streaming feature will be restricted for 90 days.
- If the user receives three warnings for non-compliance, the account will be cancelled, all videos will be removed from the account, and the user will not be able to create new accounts.

Its impact as a platform

YouTube made a big impact on global society soon after it was launched. In fact, in November 2006, Time magazine awarded it the Invention of the Year award for becoming a very popular medium for the virilization of all Internet phenomena in every aspect. Its impact has been such that it even became a showcase for all artists, singers, influencers, media personalities, and much more, making more immediate and viral the promotion of any album, film and much more, displacing the traditional promotion by CD or DVD of any material. Currently, the platform is a necessary reference for anyone looking for all audiovisual material, such as historical, musical, documentary, investigative, tutorial, and much more.

Instagram

Instagram is a platform or Social Network designed to publish and share photos and videos with other users of the network. When you publish this material, you can apply effects, filters, frames, thermal image effects, retro colors, and much more, and then share them in all your associated networks such as Facebook, twitter, Tumblr and Flickr. The main attraction of the platform is that it allows to publish photographs in square form alluding to Kodak Instamatic and Polaroid cameras, since the publication format is 16:9 (Cinema) and 4:3 (standard) because most intelligent devices and cameras use it. When this application started, in order to be able to publish a Horizontal or Vertical photo within the 4:3 parameter (standard, the only one allowed at the beginning), it was necessary to adapt them to white borders that would allow it to be adjusted and centered for publication, so that the application would not have to cut any part of said material. At present, this is no longer necessary, as you can publish it complete without further complication as the platform allows you to adjust it to the full size and orientation to not lose even a little of the image.

Instagram was launched on October 6, 2010, created by Kevin Systrom and Mike Krieguer. In 2012, this platform had more than 100 million users, and by December 2014, tripled this figure to 300 million users.

As a curious fact, Instagram was originally intended for iPhone and the entire range IOS 3.0.2 or higher, but at the beginning of 2012 it reached the Android system, by 2013 it reached Windows Phone and in 2016 it reached Windows 10.

It is important to note that at first the published videos could only last up to 15 seconds, but for version 4.0 the application updated this allowing the maximum duration to be 1 minute. To date, this company has at least 900 million active users.

By April 9, 2012, Facebook announces the acquisition of the company for at least USD 1 billion. A few months later, in December of the same year, Instagram updates its terms and conditions of privacy and use, allowing users' photos to be sold to third parties without notice or compensation from January 16, 2013, but after much criticism from consumers and important bodies, Instagram undoes the changes. Thanks to this crisis, Instagram loses a large part of its users who preferred to switch to services similar to Instagram.

Correct use of the Instagram

Each of the multimedia platforms has a beginner's guide that highlights the right way to use them and get the most out of them:

Download the application: Instagram, unlike other social networks, can only be managed through a smart device or mobile, since from a computer can only monitor the activity of it. For this reason, you must first download the application to your device in order to use it effectively and continue with the following steps.

Create your user in Instagram: When you open the application, you will see a screen with two messages: Create Account, and Login. Select "Create Account" and you will immediately have the option to create your account using your Facebook profile, cell phone number or email address. From here, you must create your username and enter your password. It is important to note that the username you choose will be the name that other network users will be able to search for and follow you to view your shared videos and photos. Then you must add your profile picture, fill in your description or biography, and complete the data form to validate all your information.

Discover new people: When you have finished creating your profile, you can start looking for people you might be interested in following to see their posts. For this, Instagram will offer you a list of account suggestions that you might be interested in following. They are usually celebrity or brand accounts, or they are simply users that Instagram located by reviewing your cell phone contact list, email account or Facebook account after linking all these accounts to your Instagram profile.

Search Instagram: Once you are on your Instagram home screen, you will be able to search for photos and post from different Instagram users. To do this you should tap the magnifying glass icon at the bottom of the screen, then type the name of the user you want to search for or the tag (Hashtag) you want to locate to view referred posts. When you type, Instagram will show you everything referred to in publications with that search word (Results).

Explore in Instagram: Here you can see all the most seen or viral trends and publications of the moment. Recommendations offered by Instagram according to your locality, people you follow, people who follow you and anything related to your interests in the platform so that you do not miss a single detail of the current trend in the network. For this you must touch the magnifying glass icon again without typing or searching anything, just browse the page discovering the posts that appear from other users or Influencers.

Upload and share a photo or video: just click on the central square icon at the bottom of the screen, there you can access your gallery or reel to view and choose the photos or videos you want to share in your post. Videos should last between 3 to 60 seconds. You can take a picture or video directly from the application and publish it immediately. You can also publish a complete album of 10 photos or videos (can be mixed) in a single post. Just select the small button that appears in the lower right corner of the photo or video selector and then select the photos or videos you want to share in a single album.

Edit photos in Instagram: when preparing to publish, you must select "Next" to access the gallery of filters and tools once you have selected the photos to be published. You can scroll to see all the options in filters available for the platform. There you can edit the brightness or contrast, the orientation of the image, and everything you want. Once this process is finished, you only have to press "Apply".

Share the photos and videos already selected: After having done all the steps described above, you must write the copy that will accompany the post. Remember that this copy is the one that accompanies in the inferior part to the photos, videos or albumen that we want to post. Try not to make wills or texts so long because the application is characterized more by the visualization of their photos or videos than by their texts. It is advisable to use and include Hashtags related to the publication so that more people interested in your tastes and in the labels placed in the post can see it. You can tag people in photos or videos, include your location and, if you want, you can share your post with the same copy to Facebook, Twitter, Tumblr or Flickr.

If you want to send or share this post only with a certain group of people, click on the "Direct" icon in the upper right corner, and choose the people with whom you want to share the publication (it can be your own publication or that of another user you follow and decide to share their material).

Tap on the "Share" button at the bottom of the screen and the post will be published in Instagram.

Creating Boomerangs: Not only can you share videos or photos, but also Boomerangs, an exclusive mode of Instagram, which consists of capturing videos in motion and are played back to front, front to back and vice versa for 6 seconds, however, the recorded material is two seconds. This gives an inverted motion effect to the video. For this, you only have to record your boomerang through the Stories of your account in the "Camera" button in the upper left corner, where you can choose the boomerang, record it and save it in your phone and then share it as a post (we explained it before).

Zoom in the photos and videos of Instagram: When the application began operating in 2010, it did not allow to zoom in on the photos to better detail them, but in 2016, and after so many requests, Instagram decides to include among its tools the function of Zoom to the different photos or videos that appear in the Activity Feed. To make the image bigger, you just have to touch with both fingers as if you were pinching to make the image bigger.

Profile in Instagram: The last icon of your lower navigation headband (with silhouette of a person or your profile picture) is the one that will direct you to your main profile where you will be able to see all the posts you have shared in your account.

Stories: This feature is similar to SnapChat, another popular social network for audiovisual messaging. To create a Story, you only have to touch the icon in the form of a camera located in the upper left corner, where the camera will open, to generate a video, photo, make an Instagram Live (direct), boomerang or a Rewind. There you can even label people who appear with you in the material, share your location, use a hashtag, place emoticons and much more.

Its impact and scope

By March 11, 2012, Instagram announced that it had more than 27 million registered users. However, Mark Zuckerberg (creator of Facebook), in September of the same year announced that they had already reached 100 million registered users.

According to Instagram parameters, by May 2012 at least 58 photos per second were uploaded, and every second a new user was registered in the application. Up to that date, a total of one billion photographs had been uploaded. On August 9, singer Elie Goulding released the videoclip of her song Anything Could Happen, which is constructed of pure photographs retouched with filters regularly used in Instagram. This clip lasted at least 4 minutes, where more than 1200 photographs were used.

In August 2017, the company indicated that it had more than 800 million active users so far.

Instagram and its Filters

At the time of making any publication, you have a wide range of filters with which you can adapt the beauty of your image to your taste. These filters are:

- **Clarendon**: Intensifies shadows and illuminate's reflections. Originally released as a video-only filter.
- **Gingham:** Wash the photos. It gives a yellowish tone when used in dark photos or a brighter, drowsy look when used in light photos.
- **Moon**: Black and white version of Gingham, with slightly more intense shadows.
- **Lark**: Desaturated reds while amplifying blues and greens brings landscapes to life.
- **Kings:** Gives photos a dusty, vintage look.
- **Juno**: Shades cold tones in green, makes warm tones stand out and whites shine.
- **Slumber**: Desaturate the image and add mist for a retro, sleepy look, with emphasis on blacks and blues.
- **Cream:** Adds a creamy appearance that both warms and cools the image.

- **Ludwig:** A light touch of desaturation that also improves light.
- **Aden:** Gives a natural look of blues and greens.
- **Perpetual**: Adds a pastel look, ideal for portraits.
- **Amaro:** Adds light to the image, with a focus in the center.
- **Mayfair**: Apply a warm pink tone, subtle vignettes to illuminate the center of the photograph, and a thin black border.
- **Rise**: Adds a "glow" to the image, with a softer illumination of the subject.
- **Hudson:** Creates a "frosty" illusion with intense shadows, cold dye and dodged center.
- **Valencia**: Fades the image by increasing the exposure and warming the colors, giving it an antique touch.
- **X-Pro II:** Increases color vitality with a golden tint, high contrast and a slight vignette added to the edges.
- **Saw:** Gives a faded and smooth appearance.
- **Willow:** A monochromatic filter with subtle purple tones and a translucent white border.
- **Lo-Fi:** Enriches color and adds strong shadows through the use of saturation and "heating" of temperature.
- **Earlybird:** Gives photographs an older appearance with a sepia tone and a warm temperature.
- **Brannan:** Increases contrast and exposure and adds a metallic dye.
- **Inkwell:** Direct change to black and white - no additional editing.

- **Hefe:** High contrast and saturation, with an effect similar to Lo-Fi but not so dramatic.
- **Nashville:** Heats the temperature, reduces contrast and increases exposure to give a slight "pink" tint, giving it a "nostalgic" air.
- **Suture:** Burn photo edges, increase reflections and shadows dramatically with a focus on purple and brown colors.
- **Toaster**: Makes the center of the image "burn" and adds a dramatic vignette.
- **Walden**: Increases exposure and adds a yellow tint.
- **1977**: With a larger exhibition of red dye that gives the photograph a pink, shiny and faded appearance.
- **Kelvin**: Increases saturation and temperature to give it a radiant "glow".
- **Stinson:** Subtle filter that illuminates the image, slightly eliminating colors.
- **Vesper.**
- **Maven.**
- **Ginza.**
- **Skyline.**
- **Dogpatch.**
- **Brooklyn.**
- **Helena.**
- **Ashby.**
- **Charmes.**

*With referential information from Wikipedia *

We cannot leave aside the filters used in the Stories, which are:

- **Rio de Janeiro:** Gives an effect of degraded colors from purple to yellow.
- **Tokyo**: Gives a black and white effect.
- **Cairo**: Gives a yellowish and vintage hue.
- **Jaipur**: Gives a pink hue and clarity.
- **New York**: Creates a dark vignette effect that highlights dark tones.
- **Buenos Aires**: It enhances the lights and saturates the dark tones.
- **Abu Dhabi**: Softens the image and enhances the yellow tones.
- **Jakarta**: Enhances the lights and gives a pale tone.
- **Melbourne**: Decreases saturation and softens the image.
- **Lakes**: Softens the image in a yellowish tone.
- **Oslo**: Enhances shadows.

*With referential information from Wikipedia *

The application is constantly updating it, including new filters, masks, and much more, to make its use more dynamic.

Associated applications

Instagram is an application that has many functionalities and seeks to make more dynamic your experience within the application. Among their associated applications, they have:

PrintingGram: A website that allows Instagram users to print their own Instagram photos in different types: magnets, calendars, photo albums, decorative plates, among others. A printing service so that *instagrammers* can turn their photos into something real.

Instagrammers: Web portal with news, utilities, applications and products related to the world of Instagram from the world's largest community of Instagram users. Its main portal is instagramers.com

Instamap: Application available for iPad that allows Instagram users to find photos referring to their location or a certain hashtag. The results can be viewed in a gallery or linked to a map.

Schedugr.am: is a web portal that allows Instagram users to schedule the publication of photographs in their accounts from a web platform, so that they do not have to worry about publishing them manually at the right time.

100 Cameras in 1: is an application available for iPhone, iPad, Windows and Android users that provides additional effects to photos, with the possibility of uploading them to Instagram.

Carousel: for Mac, offers a live broadcast of Instagram on the Mac.

Iconosquare.com: (formerly Statigr.am) is a paid application that provides personal statistics related to Instagram, including the number of followers, likes, comments, and usage statistics.

Instagram and Printing - Instaprint: offers a rental device for social gatherings that allows users to print photos on Instagram.

Printic: Offers one of the easiest ways to print and share Instagram photos from an iPhone. The images are sent in a 3x4 inch (7.62x10.16 cm) format, in an orange envelope and a message to the recipient.

Optink (optink.com): is a website that allows the creation of Instagram frames for photo call through the online platform, also allows the creation of Facebook frames, Twitter and others. It is a good physical complement for taking photographs and sharing them on social networks.

Socialmatic: is a prototype of a digital camera with a cover designed in a style identical to the Instagram icon. The camera is designed with 16GB of storage, Wi-Fi and Bluetooth. It has the ability to interact with the Instagram application and produce color prints.

SubirfotosaInstagramdesdepc: This web platform, helps you learn a little programming in order to upload photos to Instagram with Python using the Instagram API.

Grammar: is an application that offers Instagram users additional options in the application's photo album, such as: zoom out, hide photos, create lists or link different accounts.

Pro HDR: is an application for iOS and Android that merges images to get great pictures in HDR resolution.

Tweegram: is an application for iOS that converts a text, with different styles, into an image to upload to Instagram.

PicFrame: available for iOS and Android, unites different images in a single fragment.

TheShow: is an application created by Red Bull that allows you to transform your Instagram photos into a photographic exhibition as if it were a modern art gallery. Once you connect to the application website, you can download the video generated from your exposure and share it on social networks.

Flipagram: is an application that allows the creation of short videos with photographs, where the user chooses the number of photographs, the rhythm and the music of the video. These videos can be shared on other networks such as Instagram, Facebook or Twitter.

Instagrafic: available for iOS and Android, it allows the creation of a photo album with 36 photographs. This album can be shared or printed.

Instagraph Uploader: available for Symbian, S40 and Windows Phone. It allows to publish images in Instagram, and the version for Symbian and Windows Phone allows to share them in the social networks.

Instacollage: application available for iOS and Android, it allows to join the photos in more than 20 collages grids (now available the new version with 3D collages) and to add numerous filters and effects to the photos, allowing to share them directly to social networks like Instagram, Facebook, Twitter and Flickr.

Instaweather: application available for iOS and Android, allows to share besides a photo, the weather and the city where you are located directly in Instagram. This application is widely used for travel and recreation.

Boomerang: application available for IOS and Android, transforms everyday moments into fun and unexpected experiences, creates attractive short videos of continuous repetition, just look for something moving and touch a button and Boomerang will take care of the rest. The application will create a charming video from 10 photos or videos of your choice. You can share it directly on Facebook and Instagram or save it in the camera album for later publication.

InShot: application available for IOS and Android, is a professional video and photo editor, gives the option to add music and effects to any video, also trims and compresses videos.

With referential information from Wikipedia

Facebook

Facebook is an American Internet chat and instant messaging company born on February 4, 2004 by a group of students at Harvard University, where the mastermind was Mark Zuckerberg, along with Eduardo Saverin, Andrew McCollum, Dustin Moskovitz and Chris Hughes, who were roommates at Harvard University. This web platform was initially designed for interaction and chat between Harvard students themselves through a web membership, later the membership was extended to all higher education students in the Boston area, and in 2006 it was free and open to anyone over 13 years of age. In 2008 it began to be available in Spanish to continue expanding its service to more regions of the world with Internet connection.

In 2012 this company had already reached a value of 104 million dollars in the Stock Exchange Public Offering (OPV), achieving revenue through advertising ads that appeared on the screen of users of the network.

To date, Facebook has at least 2.2 billion users per month. Over the years they have developed different policies and laws for the use of their platform to maintain harmony among Internet users, such as facing the great pressure exerted by thousands of users with their *fake news*, incitement to hate, among other issues.

In 2012, the company acquired Instagram shares for at least $1 billion, and in February 2014 acquired WhatsApp instant messaging for $16 billion to complete its worldwide communications monopoly.

In 2017, Facebook had a net income of at least US$40.653 billion, and currently has 30,275 direct employees throughout the company. The company also has translations in all the world's languages, as it has a presence in all regions of the planet, with the exception of some countries that have blocked access to the network for political, ethnic, among others.

How can we use this tool?

In this section we explain how to use Facebook step by step:

1. Create a Facebook account or membership

Creating an account is quite simple, but you must fill out the entire form correctly. Access the official Facebook platform page (Facebook.com).

When you enter the home page, you will see a screen or tab with a message that will allow you to log in to Facebook using your email or phone number and password. This section is exclusive for users who already have their membership in the social network, so far you will be close to this, but not yet.

Under the upper left headband, where you can log in, you have a section that says, "Create Account", and then a small form to complete. In this form you must complete your personal data: Name, Surname, Telephone, e-mail address, date of birth, sex and password. Once the task is finished, press the "Register" button. It is important to emphasize that for Facebook you must place your real personal data, that is, if once you register your data you want to impersonate them, it can be considered a crime. By registering definitively, you are accepting all of Facebook's terms and conditions of use, so it's a good idea to review all of that information before continuing with your membership application and registration.

2. Find friends on Facebook

The intention of this platform is to simplify communications between you and your acquaintances around the world, in addition to meeting many more people in the attempt. In this function, you can locate all your acquaintances, family and friends, so that they can interact online, share moments, photos and much more in their profiles so that all their common friends can see it. In order to enjoy this, Facebook has an algorithm that allows you to show a suggestion from friends based on various sources, such as your email, list of cell phone contacts, acquaintances on sites where you can frequent and have registered in your profile, among other sources. Once you have this list of suggestions, you can decide yourself who you want to connect with and send your friend request, if you don't want to, you don't do anything, and nothing happened.

After sending the friend request, you will have to wait a few minutes, hours, or days (depending on the next connection of the person or friend to whom you sent the friend request) for the person to accept or reject your request to be friends on this social network. Similarly, if you want to search for a specific person or account, you can do so by typing their name in the search engine that you see on the top of the page, where all accounts registered on Facebook with the name or similar names appear.

3. Add content to your profile

Your profile on the Facebook network can function as your cover letter to all your friends, acquaintances and not so acquaintances, so they can know and see what you share, your interests, comments and any content you want to add to your profile.

To add content, you must access your account profile through the icon with your photo and your name in the upper right-hand corner of the window, right next to the start button. After you're on that screen, you'll see a box with the question "What are you thinking?", where you can post a comment, photo, video, news, and much more. This material will be seen by all your friends on their respective TimeLine, where you can also give him "Like", comment or share on his profile so that his friends (even those who are not yours) can see it. In this box you can even share your location, an event and invite your friends to attend, indicate a feeling or activity, and much more.

4. What are your friends doing on Facebook?

As we mentioned in the previous item, when you publish any content in your account, your friends can see it on their timeline. To enjoy the content your friends, share, just go to the "Home" tab to locate your profile of news and updates. There you will be able to enjoy the most recent posts or publications of your friends on the net, and you will be able to slide down to continue seeing more and more publications thanks to Facebook's algorithm to see the most popular ones according to the "Like" and comments you may have. If you want to see the news in chronological order, you can go to the "Most Recent" section in the right headband.

In each publication you will be able to make several types of interaction:

- **"Like" button:** When you slide the mouse over the icon without clicking, several reaction options will be displayed on that publication, such as "I love it, I'm angry, I fall in love, among others. This function allows you to show how you feel about the post you are viewing.

- **Comment**: Each publication has space to know the opinion of those who see it, expressing the comments they wish to leave. You only have to press "Comment" and there write what you consider about the post, even tagging other friends so they can see it. It should be noted that comments must be respectful and not contain discriminatory language or incite hatred or violence as this may be a crime for Facebook and he is entitled to cancel the comment, and even your account (this clause is in the terms and conditions).

- **Share**: If you liked that publication very much, and you think that more people should see and enjoy it as much as you do, you can press the "Share" button to share it on your page as a direct post, or write a comment on your profile referring to that post.

When you click on "Share", a menu with different options is displayed where: you can share on your profile directly for all your friends to see and interact as well; send it as a message; or share it on a friend's profile or on another page.

5. Chat privately on Facebook

The Facebook community gives you the option of communicating and interacting privately with your friends on the platform or with anyone even if you don't have them as a friend, that is, without anyone else being able to read or know what they are talking about. If you want to chat, just click the "Messages" button on the top right bar (with the symbol of a message cloud), or on the bottom right in the "Chat" menu where it also tells you the number of friends connected at that time. At that moment all the most recent contacts and chats will be opened, where you will be able to select the contact with whom you want to establish communication.

In this drop-down menu you will see the option "Request Messages", where all the messages received by people who are not your friends on Facebook, but only you will have the option to decide whether to accept the chat or not.

6. Do you know how to create an event on Facebook?

If you have an event in mind and want your friends to see or attend it, such as a birthday party, meeting, etc. you just have to click on the "Home" tab, and then, on the left side of the screen, on the word "Events", then click on "+Create Event", there you will choose between creating a private event for only the people you invite directly, or creating a public event so that any user can see it and search for it even if it is not in your friends list.

When you choose one of these options, a menu will be displayed in which you will have to complete all the relevant information about the event, i.e., the name of the event, when and where it will be, and its description.

In addition to all this, you can choose a photo or video that heads the event, where you can also customize the invitation according to your tastes and preferences.

Once you have created the event, and sent the corresponding invitations, you will be able to see who will attend, who will not attend, or who may attend, making it a very practical way to organize small, medium or large events, and confirm the attendance of your guests in a more practical way.

7. Creating a Facebook Page

Maybe you have a brand that you want to create a presence on Facebook to market more to users of this social network, and that's why you want to create a fan page or commercial profile on the network, for this carries out the following steps:

Go to the "Home" screen, click on the "Pages" icon on the left side of the screen, and then on the green "Create Page" button.

Once in this phase, you must choose the use of this page: promote a place, local business, brand, product, defend a cause or create a community based on a specific theme.

You must select the most appropriate option and continue to complete all the information requested step by step until this process is complete. At the end of it all, you can invite all your friends on Facebook to like your page and get more interaction.

8. Create a group on Facebook

Facebook groups are communities of debate among members of the same, where they exchange information, ideas, or products of different users. For the Facebook platform "the groups are the ideal option to concretize many topics and be in contact with the people you want. Share photos and videos, have conversations, make plans, and more.

To create a group on Facebook, it is important to be clear about the need for that group. Once you have the idea, go to the "Home" screen of your profile, on the left-hand side click on "Groups" and then click on "Create Group". There it will open a window in which you must enter the name of the group, and add some people to open it, then you can choose the privacy or the type of privacy you want. There are three options:

- **Public group**: anyone can see the group, the members and their publications.
- **Closed group**: anyone can search for the group and see who belongs to it, but only members can see the publications.

- **Secret group**: only members can search the group and see the publications.

Then you can manage who signs in and who doesn't, to this group.

9. How to deactivate your Facebook account?

To deactivate an account, follow these steps: click on the arrow icon in the top bar of the page to the right, right next to the question mark. Click on "Settings", select "General", "Edit", "Manage Account", then more options will appear: At the end of all of them, you will read "Deactivate Account", if you select it, Facebook will ask you to confirm the decision to close the account, and then delete your name, photo and all the content you shared in your account for at least 60 days, if in 60 days you do not reactivate your account, it will be permanently deleted from its system.

Facebook and its associates

Facebook has other proprietary applications that allow you to expand your user experience to devices other than computers.

Facebook Messenger: The Facebook chat service that allows you to write messages, and even voice calls between network users, but only limited to iOS and Android system.

Poke: An application for "ephemeral" messages. This application is not part of Messenger and requires both contacts to have it downloaded. It was released in May 2014, and replaced by Slingshot which, basically, is the same with the difference that it also sends and receives "ephemeral" photos and videos (Available since June 2014).

Page Manager: The application that allows you to manage a page quickly.

Facebook Groups: Almost the same as the "Page Manager" application, but with groups.

Facebook Lite: It is the Facebook application for mobile phones, but weighs less, approximately 2MB for computers with little memory space. It uses 2g networks and slow connections. It is suitable for Android phones with older versions.

Can we monetize our Facebook management?

Many people seek to make the most of their social network accounts by charging money for their publications with brand recommendations, content visualization, etc. But really with Facebook you cannot, because with its algorithm and its platform that they can only publish content to their friends in their profile, makes it complicated that their publications are viral, and this way we can say that there are no influencers in

Facebook. Contrary to this, if you want to promote your personal brand, company, product or message, you must acquire some of the marketing plans or advertising that Facebook offers, where it assures you a specific amount of interaction with Facebook users in relation to their interests, for example, if you seek to promote your brand, and this is a car dealership, Facebook will show this publication to people who have visited a dealership on the network, car parts stores, among other interests, to make your message more effective and viral. Facebook campaigns tend to be more effective when you promote your brand with a brand profile on Facebook such as FanPage.

Is it worth measuring the indicators of Like, Comments or Shared on Facebook?

Only if you do it as a brand or company, but as a user or "Influencer" not, as mentioned above, you are not really going to increase the number of followers or views of a material by the number of Likes or comments of your publication, since this network is more to share among friends, unlike other social networks that is more to share with a specific sector or public called Followers. However, if you have a brand or FanPage of your company on Facebook, you can moderately increase interaction with your audience by posting material that your FanPage followers are interested in and want to share with their friends by tagging them in that post, but you cannot monetize that interaction in your favor.

Conclusion

Social networks are an incredible tool to communicate to the masses in a global way, at the reach of a click and at any time. The most important thing is that you must understand and learn the purpose of each platform, because if you apply the use in these platforms differently to the purpose for which they were created, you will have bad results and fail immediately.

For example, we already know that the Instagram community is a community to share audiovisual material or content, such as videos and photos through its Feed, or its Stories, with a small footer or page that allows you to complement the information or idea of the material you are sharing in it, and you can even make live transmissions through Instagram live at the time you like, and read the comments of your followers connected at that time. In this community it is no use sharing so much written content, as it will not have the same impact as audiovisual or photographic content.

Facebook, on the other hand, is a *blogging* community where users can share mixed content, videos, photos and comments on the network, as well as news, live chat between friends and much more. It is ideal for those who want to have everything mixed in one place, however, and although its impact on the masses has been maintained throughout its more than 10 years of operation, is known as the community for the elderly, as young people under 25 or 30 years prefer to consume the content of Instagram or Twitter.

YouTube offers only high-quality videos of any type of content, such as music videos, documentaries, audio video podcasts, and much more, with a worldwide impact, reference and preference for all network users, regardless of age. Content on this platform can quickly become viral if it is high quality content, especially if it is unusual, novel or fun.

Social Media Marketing 2019-2020: Volume 3

How to Build Your Personal Brand to Become an Influencer by Leveraging Facebook, Twitter, YouTube & Instagram

By

Income Mastery

INTRODUCTION

We will begin this study with the most important question: What is Instagram? If you already know the application and have used it, take this chapter as a general description of everything you know so far. Instagram is a mobile application for sharing photos, videos and other visual content. Now they'll ask themselves: What makes you so different from, say, your older brother Facebook? Obviously, you can share photos and videos on Facebook as well, but what made this application different from day one is the fact that it includes good, quality, surprising and attractive content. Basically, Instagram is something like commercial photoshoots or magazine covers. Even its official "About Us" section says that the purpose of the platform is to capture and share important moments, so it's no wonder Instagram has become the ultimate visual storytelling venue for everyone from celebrities, newsrooms and brands, to teenagers, musicians and anyone with a creative passion. Alright, now that we've made clear what Instagram is, here's the answer to the question of why you should use it. Instagram is a community of more than 1 billion people around the world. Instagram allows you to connect with people in a way Facebook, Twitter, YouTube or Snapchat could never. And, if you do it right, it could become your main channel among all the other social networks.

HOW TO START WITH INSTAGRAM?

Because Instagram works as a mobile application, you'll need your phone or tablet and a few minutes to set everything up. Once you have downloaded the application to your phone, you will need to fill in a couple of mandatory blank fields. It is suggested that you choose a primary email address that is used by the person in charge in case you have a problem with your account (for example, if you forget your password). In the "Full name" bar, type your name or the name of your brand.

Make sure the username you choose is your own without strange characters: if your name is John Smith, don't use @ju4n_p3r3z1235 as your username because it looks like spam and people will have a hard time finding you. The next thing is to choose a secure password, one that's hard to discover. Again, quite obvious, but worth mentioning: if your password is "juan1234" you will probably be hacked. Your password for Instagram, as for any other social network, should contain letters, numbers and random characters to be more secure. Write it down in a safe place or memorize it. Remember that you can always request a new Instagram password from your email address if you forget it.

Configuring your profile

Now that you have your account, you can continue with your profile picture. First of all, you must have a profile picture. This is non-negotiable. It doesn't look good or professional to leave it blank. Depending on what you do, it would be nice to have something related to your personal brand or logo. Once you have chosen the correct profile picture, be sure to fill in the name bar as well. By this I mean the real "Name" field in the Settings tab of your profile, not the Instagram username.

Why is this important? Well, your name and your username are the only fields that Instagram considers in search queries, which means that you must make sure that the name you use in your Instagram biography is the one your followers and clients are looking for. Again, it is recommended to use the same name that you used in the username. The "Instagram biography" is a brief description bar at the top of your profile that serves as a box of information about who you are, what you do, what you're offering and should be written in a way that makes people want to interact with you and follow you. Think about what sets you apart from your competition: Do you have a unique set of special products or services that might be of interest to your followers?

This information should definitely be in your Instagram biography to serve as an introduction, but it can also determine whether people will decide to follow your account or not. If they don't follow you, they won't see your updates and they're less likely to work with you. Make sure you write a good, informative biography! What you can really work on are the keywords that should be included to reflect your values and those of your target audience. Put yourself in the position of your ideal client for a moment and think about what an Instagram account would do for you: What would you like to see every time you log into Instagram? And what keywords will resonate more with your target audience? The use of keywords helps users better understand who you are, what you have to offer and whether your account is relevant to them. Don't be shy about emojis either: they attract attention, so feel free to use some that make sense, but don't exaggerate. The next thing you need to put in your profile is the link to your website. Once people find out about your account, they'll want to know more about you and what you do. Be sure to give them access through your Instagram account to your website. Currently, Instagram gives users a link that can be clicked on in your profile, and it would be a shame not to take advantage of it.

This link can take people to your home page or blog, but if you have an e-commerce business, you may need to update this link from time to time to send your followers to your latest announcements or promotions. Obviously, you will have to indicate it in your Instagram subtitles (we will see that later). In addition to having a link to the website, such as an Instagram account related to the company, it would be advisable to share your email in the biography. Make it easy for your followers to contact you if they have any questions.

Alright, let's summarize everything:

After setting up your account by choosing the correct username, you should upload a profile image that gives your target audience an idea of who you are and what you do. Then, choose the correct name that will be visible in bold for each new person who logs into your Instagram account. Write a biography where you talk more about yourself and target your niche audience using keywords, link to your website, blog or online store. Find a way for your followers to communicate with you by sharing an email address.

Once you've completed all of these steps, you're ready to start publishing content.

GUIDE FOR INSTAGRAM INFLUENCERS

It may seem like the influential marketing trend has emerged from nowhere, but it has actually been brewing for several years, largely due to the increase in ad blocking technology in online media. The changing purchase patterns of millennials (those 18-34 year-olds who have come of age in the 21st century) have had a major impact on the way brands generate awareness and increase engagement, driving the increased influencer marketing movement. Millennials usually want to examine things and come to their own conclusions. The atypical millennial does not always trust what other people promote. This makes influencers their main source of brand information, as opposed to more traditional methods of advertising and television broadcasting. Millennials are also avid "cable cutters", they give up television and use social networks as their main source of news and other information. This consolidates influencers in their digital worlds.

INSTAGRAM FOR INFLUENCERS

Influencer Marketing started with popular bloggers several years ago and has now spread to other channels such as Instagram and YouTube, largely due to its visual appeal and its ability to instantly connect with readers. In addition, studies show that brands retain 37 percent more customers achieved through "word of mouth" than through traditional advertising, and influencer marketing is a high form of word of mouth. The numbers also support this theory, as Instagram is one of the most popular social networking platforms with just over 600 million active users. Brands work with influential Instagram people to promote their businesses, launch new products, share corporate culture, establish brand stories and more.

TYPES OF MARKETING CAMPAIGNS FOR INSTAGRAM INFLUENCERS

Instagram influencers have many opportunities to promote content in different types of campaigns. Here is a quick overview of Instagram's common influencer campaigns:

Brand content: When companies want to share their brand stories, they often drive brand content in collaboration with influential people who will deliver it in their own styles, as their followers expect.

Product placement: sometimes brands will want to present their products through a channel or platform of influence. The influencer will have the opportunity to show the product within their style, which will lead to greater awareness of the product and the brand.

General creative campaigns: sometimes influencers are free to create content in the form of images, videos and more, and the brand only gives them a general theme or concept. This allows the personality of the influencer to emerge, all the while increasing the likings and participations of the followers.

Hashtag campaigns: brands can gain momentum by running hashtag campaigns, especially if they become viral. Hashtags are excellent for initiating conversations and are very socially actionable, which increases their overall value.

Increase followers: Sometimes brands will execute campaigns with social networking influencers in an attempt to increase their number of followers. By aligning with an influencer who has a highly engaged audience, a brand can dramatically increase its social exposure and increase its own fanbase.

Contests: Brands can interact with influential people in order to promote a contest, sweepstakes or gifts that will generate conversation and interest. When an influencer participates, this will dramatically increase the reach and exposure of the contest, creating a lot of goodwill and, hopefully, new followers for the brand.

STARTING AS AN INSTAGRAM INFLUENCER

Instagram is huge in terms of influential marketing, and it is relatively easy to get started. But there are some things influencers can do to prepare for success.

First, refine the niche. What makes it unique? What are you passionate about? What product or cause can you back up without fail? Influential people need to live their niche, as it defines what they publish on Instagram. It is critical that the passion of an influencer shines in every publication. Authenticity is critical.

Second, determine your objectives: Why do you want to be an Instagram influencer? What do you want to achieve by working with an influencer? What do you expect to achieve through your influencer activity? As best as you can, define your objectives when you start in terms of target audience, objectives, measurement of success, etc. Your influencer objectives are likely to change as your activity increases, and you will need to adjust your objectives as your influencer marketing ramps up.

BEST PRACTICES FOR POSTING

In the excitement of launching your influencers marketing efforts at Instagram, you may be willing to start publishing anything and everything just to get content in the hope of finding some followers. Not so fast. Just as you need to define your niche and overall objectives in order to become influential, it is also essential to plan out your publication activities.

Telling a story

Storytelling is the foundation of any great content marketing initiative, and your influential publications should be no different. Great content means a great story, and influential salespeople must become great storytellers. Storytelling has been an important form of communication for centuries because people can easily relate to each other and enjoy each other's experiences. There is something powerful about the emotional pull of a great story, and intelligent influencers can translate that pull into sales and customer loyalty.

So how do you create a story that appeals to people when you talk about a product or company? The first thing to consider is that a company is the 3 people that make up the business, not just an organization or a building. People find it easier to relate to human interest stories than anything else. The key is to make your business interesting to humans. Studies have shown that human brains experience neuronal coupling with whatever a narrator shares; in fact, they are at the same wavelength. Empathy is created by listening to someone share a story, and the listener may feel the pleasure or pain of the narrator. This gives brands the support they need to be able to share their value propositions through stories that can relate to their readers. It's easier to connect with compelling stories than with dry features and benefit checklists of products and solutions. Influencers who can change the corner from selling to sharing will be the ones who win in the end.

No shortcuts

Quality rules with Instagram publications. That applies to content and images, but it also applies to the frequency of your publications. It is better to publish fewer times and have authentic and relevant content for your followers than to publish unrelated content many times a day in the hope of getting some more followers. People will find you and follow you if your publications have a tone of authenticity. Be someone you can trust publishing just for the sake of publishing never really works.

No one can be that fascinating several times a day, right? Therefore, make sure that when you publish, you provide relevant information. One of your main roles as an influencer is to build trust, and you can't do that if you constantly publish irrelevant things. Make your publications matter and your followers will reward you with their loyalty.

Perfect image

Let's face it: photos rule in Instagram. It is therefore essential that the images you publish are of the highest quality. If your shots are low resolution, blurry, silenced or something less than dynamic, they will show that you simply don't care about quality, and that's the social death of any influencer. If you can afford it, invest in a digital SLR camera for the best quality photos. Do not think of this as an expense, but rather as an investment. If you plan to become an important influencer on Instagram, high quality images will dominate your world. However, many smartphones have good camera functions and may work well until you're ready to upgrade. There are Instagram guides to create excellent images, but as a general rule, avoid flash photography. Shoot in natural light because it's more visually appealing. Exceptions may be product photography, where you need studio-type configurations to adequately display your products. Experiment with composition as well. People are attracted to images that have interesting perspectives and angles. However, don't do anything that doesn't seem natural to you, as your discomfort will appear in your photos and that's the last thing you want.

Be sure to think square when composing and cropping images. Instagram works in square format, so if you remember that when you take photos, you will be happier with the final result because your images will be created with the correct proportion.

HOW TO MONETIZE YOUR CONTENT THROUGH A CREATIVE MARKET LIKE IZEAX

Instagram is a dynamic social networking platform and can be a lot of fun for everyone involved. But it's also a great tool for making money: just look at all the fashion, food, entertainment, sports, DIY, fitness and other influential people who have created wealth simply by delving deeper into what they love in Instagram.

The amount of money influencers can earn from marketing depends on a few factors, including the activity rate of the influencer, the scope of work, the influencer niche and its scope. The amount that an Instagram installer (Instagram influencer) makes may depend on whether a brand will fit the audience of followers of the influencer.

It is known that Instagram influencers can make up to thousands of dollars per publication with brand sponsored publications and the trend shows promise to continue on a similar path. Influencer marketing on Instagram can be big business for both the influential and the brand, so it is important to make the best possible combination with the influential character and brand personality.

Once the relationship between brand and influence is established, the sky is the limit. Instagrammers can earn good money to attend brand-sponsored events, travel to interesting destinations or even document a particularly moving experience. Those who are interested in influencer marketing, especially for airlines, hotels and tourism departments, earn the best dollar in pursuit of their influencer objectives.

As mentioned, one way is to create sponsored publications, which are paid for by the brands you align with.

Companies often resort to influencers to obtain content repeatedly, which can be very lucrative for the brand and for influencing. Some brands that have made profitable connections with influential people include Birchbox, Johnnie Walker, Taco Bell, PlayStation, Red Bull and many more. One of the byproducts of influencer marketing and social networking has been the establishment of influencer marketing agencies that help influencers and brands find each other to create visibility and profitability.

Another popular way to monetize your Instagram content is to subscribe to accounts with creator markets such as IZEAx, which can help facilitate sponsorships between brands and creators. Your marketplace technology can promote you and help you get presentations to companies that like your content and are interested in buying it. Aligning yourself with a market of creators can accelerate the growth of your recognition and help you create wealth as an Instagram influencer.

The world of social networking influencers has created a whole new way of looking at brands and has turned celebrities into ordinary people who simply have passion and attractive personalities. As the social networking landscape continues to transform and evolve, one thing will remain: the influence of people who share their passion with authenticity and who provide relevant information for their followers.

The digital age demands a more sophisticated channel for word of mouth marketing, which is the summed-up definition of influencer marketing, and Instagram is a great vehicle for leveraging initiatives created by marketing experts. Instagram is the perfect vehicle for influencer marketing because of its incredible visual ability to share stories.

In addition, each of these stories, images and videos creates actionable data to be analyzed and used for improvement.

In general, Instagram is popular because it is very easy to use. It is also highly actionable, which means that influencers can build communities of followers that increase customer loyalty, visibility and profit. Brands increasingly understand this, and the role of influencers is firmly rooted not only in the social network landscape, but also in the hearts of those who follow them. It's a very rewarding journey for those who take up the challenge.

HOW TO INCREASE YOUR FOLLOWERS

Starting out as an influencer on Instagram may seem a little daunting. You want to have a lot of followers and sometimes it takes a little time to get there. It's nothing to worry about.

If you follow a few basic steps, you will increase your follower count organically and reap the rewards for your patience.

1. MAKE YOUR PROFILE PUBLIC: This may seem elementary, but while setting up your Instagram account, make sure that your profile is visible to everyone. Staying private as an influencer goes against the very nature of what you are trying to achieve, so don't make this simple mistake.

2. PUBLISH EVERY DAY: Generally, only a beautiful and relevant image will suffice, but stay active with your account. People will evaluate their interest in your topic and look for your publications because they are meaningful and interesting. There's no need to bombard

your followers with quick publications. A safe and constant presence is the key.

3. IMAGE DESCRIPTIONS: Every time you upload a photo, be sure to create a title or description to help your followers understand what they are seeing. Tagging people in your comment will help increase reach. All you have to do is type the @ sign followed by the person's Instagram username.

4. REQUEST COMMENTS: When you post a new image, ask people for their opinion about it. People love to give their opinions, and when they share, their followers will also notice what they are commenting on, will see your publications, and ideally start following you as well. Conversely, if you are asked to comment on someone else's post, do so. It's a great way to build relationships and increase your fan base.

5. USA HASHTAGS: Hashtags can be very important to add new followers to your Instagram account. When you provide a hashtag tag, you help people interested in that topic to find it and hopefully comment on its publication or register to follow it. For example, if you're an influential chocolate candy maker, some hashtags like #chocolate, #chocolatecandy and #chocolatebliss will attract those interested in chocolate candy to your publications. You don't need to use too many, just some that you consider are the most relevant and can attract other people.

What to publish?

Since its launch in 2010, Instagram has quickly become the favorite social network of many people, which is not surprising. Here's the thing. Everybody's on Facebook these days. I have it, of course, but my mother has it, my aunt, my cousins. Every person I went to school with has it. That person I once met in the bathroom of a nightclub has it: everyone. The problem with Facebook is that most people have the feeling that they NEED to accept friend requests from everyone they have talked to. Before you know it, your feed is full of photos of babies of people you don't really care about, vacation photos of acquaintances whose last name you wouldn't know if you ever saw them anywhere on the street, and political comments from your distant relatives or who bothered you since you were a kid. With Instagram, it's different: You don't have to follow anyone you don't want. The main point is that everyone is there to see beautiful images, get inspired, and then get back to their daily lives. Another key point to remember is that Instagram is favored both by millennials who love the Instagram content format first, and by marketers seeking to create branded content in collaboration with influential people on social networks. With the popularity of Instagram, today there are people who turned their influence into a career. Working with brands, creating content with them and / or for them, depending on their number of followers, is a fairly expensive business in the digital world. This brings me to my first tip for you if you want to conquer Instagram successfully.

CONTENT IS KING:

Digital marketers love this phrase. It has been said so many times before, and one would think everyone already knows how to implement it in their strategies, but unfortunately, that is not the case. Many brands realize that they should be on Instagram, so they set up their profile, post a couple of photos, add a dozen hashtags and then give up if, within a month, they don't have thousands of people following them, and social network influencers aren't filling them with affection or waiting online to collaborate with them. That's not how it works. With Instagram, you need to think long term. You need to create incredible, visually beautiful and relevant content for your followers. One, ten or even 50 images are not enough. When someone first discovers their Instagram profile, they will most likely scroll up and down, because they want to evaluate whether their content type is something they would like to see in their Instagram feed. Invest in creative ideas, brainstorm with people from creative industries, get inspired through other profiles (but don't copy!), think outside the box. Instagram offers you a lot: photos, videos, galleries with a slide show of up to 10 photos, Boomerangs that are basically videos that act as GIFs, Stories of Instagram that disappear after 24 hours ... If you really want to get something out of your Instagram, hire professionals who will think of a thoughtful strategy, who will be familiar with your brand identity and who will take into account that publishing stock photos on Instagram will not give you anything.

ENGAGEMENT TOOLS IN SOCIAL NETWORKS

Instagram is incredible for brand awareness, but also for commitment. How many times in the last two years have you read somewhere that certain Instagram publications became viral? "Internet can't cope" and "People had a breakdown" are just some of the most commonly used lines in titles when websites report an Instagram publication that generates a lot of commitment: I like it, comments, reposting, etc. How does that look in practice? Here's a great example of Forrester: Red Bull posted a video of a unique half-snowboard tube on Facebook and Instagram. A few days later, they noticed that the 43 million Facebook fans of the brand had liked the video only 2,600 times (a rate of 0.006% of I like per fan), while their 1.2 million Instagram fans had liked the video more than 36,000 times (3% of I like per fan). The point is: yes, you should definitely have a Facebook page if you are a serious brand in the 21st century. But, if your brand lacks social engagement on Facebook or Twitter, try Instagram. Once again, if you want your followers to relate to your brand, give them quality and relevant content. Don't assume that Instagram users will get involved simply because you are on Instagram, posting photos. So how can people decide who to follow and who to commit to? Well, that brings us to number 3 ...

THEME IS QUEEN.

If content is king, the theme of your Instagram is queen. Or Khaleesi, whichever you prefer. However, it is immensely important to emphasize once again: aesthetics is the key to success at Instagram. Choose your niche and fulfill it. Whether you're posting photos of food, fashion items, or promoting a particular lifestyle, make sure all your photos have the same "ambiance". Don't think that showing the same editing style won't limit it either; just make sure all your photos have the same brightness, saturation and filters in common. For example, if you choose to combine bright and eye-catching colors, forget about mixing black and white images.

Here's another great example: Katie Gong is an interior designer and artist who uses her Instagram to promote her carpentry business. As you can see, her Instagram profile is beautifully composed with simplicity, warm tones and browns with occasional white tones. All in all, it works out beautifully, so it's no surprise that Katie has managed to get more than 18k followers on Instagram. If you don't really have a niche, but still want your Instagram feed to look attractive, then use a filter on all your photos. Forget brightness, saturation, contrast and other settings. Choose a filter you like best and then add it to each image you publish. You can play with the amount of filter you want in your images. It is possible that somewhere you want to add 100% complete, but in other photos you will add only 20% of the filter. That way, your feed will look more cohesive and combine better.

MISTER MONOTONY

Make sure it's not monotonous. That's one of the most difficult things to work out: finding out how to make an individual photo look great along with all your other previously published photos. Here's a little tip that helped me a lot: a preview of your feed using other applications. For example, for my personal Instagram, I use the VSCO application for image editing, which also allows me to see how this particular image combines with others that I have uploaded and previously published. VSCO isn't the only application that lets you do that. The Later application is another great example that you can use which, apart from previewing your feed, is also quite useful for programming your photos in Instagram.

Unless you are completely dedicated to a niche, be sure not to post two images of the same thing side by side. For example, suppose you own a small business that produces organic food and want to achieve better brand awareness through Instagram. Posting images of organic foods in your diet is excellent, but keep in mind that it is not good practice to post two images showing red apples side by side. Instead, separate these two images with one or three photos, never two. Why, you ask? Well, that way you avoid having two pictures of apples on top of each other in a column.

COMMON MISTAKES AND HOW TO AVOID THEM

You must make sure to optimize your profile as much as possible to gain followers, keep them and delight them with excellent content. This chapter will cover the top 10 mistakes made by brands in Instagram and why you should learn from them to have a successful Instagram profile. So, let's dig!

The first mistake made by brands on Instagram is bad profile optimization. Pay attention to the following: I mentioned all this at the beginning but let us emphasize on it once again. If you don't have a profile picture, followers are less likely to follow you for one simple reason: they can't see what your brand has to offer. As a profile image, brands often use their logos, and we approve of this practice. Use your logo as a profile image and make sure it looks good and centered. Another mistake is a bad description of your brand or, worse, not having a description at all. The description in your biography must be interesting and attractive. Don't just describe your products or services and make them boring as hell. Instead, tell users about your mission, your vision, or even your brand philosophy. Tell them why you are doing what you are doing and how you are doing it. Don't write a complete story, choose your words carefully and make it legible. Also, don't forget a link to your website in the biography description. This is crucial if you want to attract traffic to your website through Instagram.

You can put a link to your website or simply a particular product or service you are talking about that week. This will be explained later. Setting up your profile privately is the worst mistake you can make. If you set your profile to private, users won't be able to see your profile instantly. This is a decisive factor, Description of the profile image and link in biography, Configuration of the profile.

BAD PROFILE OPTIMIZATION

With a private profile, you're preventing users from viewing your content until you approve their request to follow you. Imagine yourself in this situation. Would you buy some apples if you couldn't get into the fruit store? Would you wait for someone to open the store? That's the point of allowing your users to see what you do the moment they find their way to your profile. Put your profile in public and let users explore it. This will make them follow you according to your content and that's the kind of followers you want.

BAD IMAGE OPTIMIZATION

This is one of the most common mistakes made by brands in Instagram. People, you must to learn what Instagram is in order to be successful! It's about images, and you know what they say: a good image is worth a thousand words. Take your time and learn how to use it. But, as we are trying to inform you about some of the worst mistakes made by brands on Instagram, we would like to highlight the ones that make us feel ashamed: low resolution or discolored images.

See the best image sizes in Instagram even before creating a profile. There is nothing worse than seeing an image that has low resolution and does not fit the Instagram sizes. Although you can now publish vertical and horizontal images, Instagram still loves square-shaped images. The higher the resolution of your images, the more credible and professional they will look. It doesn't matter if you have a small or large brand, pay attention to your images. In addition, Instagram provides all types of filters, but be careful. Don't use filters that spoil the colors because it just doesn't look good. If you want to be at the top of the game, you can use other photo-editing applications to make your images look stunning and to get that "wow" effect. We highly recommend VSCO, Snapseed and Hyperlapse, because you can make your photos and videos stand out.

This part is important for you to understand if you want to succeed at Instagram. You're probably wondering why we emphasize on this part when it seems so simple. But there are many brands that think that the content has to be very long. Wrong! Would you like to scroll through pages and pages of text? Therefore, keep in mind the

"Golden Rule": stay away from long texts and optimize them so that followers don't have to use their thumbs to scroll down and read everything you wrote. This rule depends on your brand's industry. So, if you are a beginner, explore other similar and more experienced brands in Instagram and take their example. We know that some days you just don't have time to create amazing content.

Sometimes you have to settle for not-so-perfect content in order to stay within your plan. But there is one mistake that brands often make in Instagram: re-publishing old content or, worse, making their publications look the same. Think of this from the point of view of the followers, and you will realize that this is unacceptable for a good and attractive profile. So, sit back and brainstorm what kind of content you can publish over a long-term period. Don't think it's a waste of time, it will be worth it when you see how the followers react. Followers appreciate creativity very much and are much more likely to interact with creative and surprising content than with boring one.

BAD WRITING

This applies to all brands that are killing Instagram with its "buy me, buy me!" content and make it annoying as hell. If you sell products and want to have successful traffic on Instagram, don't try to sell things: people want to bond with your brand. Lifestyle content is the best way to connect with followers. Show them what your office looks like, who works there, what values you have, what your philosophy is or what you like to do. A little selfie from time to time is desirable, but don't do it all over selfies. Again, think like a follower, not a brand!

LACK OF CREATIVITY

From time to time, you come across some fun photos, videos or something you really like. You feel the need to share it with your followers and make them laugh as if it made you laugh. But remember, this is also a mistake. This type of content is complicated, as you don't want to link your profile to content that isn't of real value to followers. For example, imagine you sell shoes and create content related to your products, create lifestyle content that is also connected to the brand, care for followers and then publish a video of a fun dog out of nowhere. See what's wrong here? We understand your intention, and it's fine, but don't publish it in your brand profile. Publish it in your personal profile. This is also something that depends on the industry you're in, so think about it in an industry context.

THE RIGHT TIME TO PUBLISH

When you don't have a clear plan to publish in Instagram, you're doomed. Imagine it from your followers' point of view. How can you expect followers to trust you and have a positive image of your brand if you publish content from time to time? If you plan to publish when you want, forget it. This will not work on Instagram or any other social network. Plan out the days when you will publish your content and follow it. That way, followers will know that you are credible, reliable, and more likely to follow. We can't tell you the exact best time of publication, but the best advice we can give you is to pay attention to the reactions of your followers and look at the Statistics with weekly analyses. The good news is that you can optimize your publication time to get the most out of I like and a good reach by looking at the information that Instagram has already provided you with. Play with the publication times at the beginning, and after a while and with a fair number of followers, you should be able to see when to publish according to the most likes get at a given time. The story doesn't end there, you have to follow it constantly and adjust it as your page grows.

USE OF HASHTAGS:

We are aware that brands often misuse hashtags and do not understand their value. Hashtags are there for a reason. It's not just looking good or making up some words you can think of. Hashtags represent symbols or codes that make web search engines understand and categorize images in Instagram. That way, when users search for a term you copied, they are shown its content. Beware of hashtags and don't go crazy with them inventing meaningless words. Choose them carefully and make sure they fit your content. If you decide to make your own hashtag with your brand name, keep it and publish it in each content.

FEAR OF FOLLOWERS

Followers are your friends, not enemies. Remember this and don't be afraid to interact with them. Brands generally publish content on Instagram on a regular basis, pay attention to as many details as possible and simply forget to interact with their followers. Look, having an Instagram profile is not just about publishing high quality content and good copywriting, it's also about interacting. Don't miss the opportunity to interact with your followers. This does not mean that you should be on Instagram 24 hours a day, 7 days a week, but it does mean that you should check your profile several times a day. By doing this, you will be able to see comments, mentions and likes on time and react to them in real time. Followers like to be appreciated and to have a sense of connection with the brands. You want your followers to like you and interact with you to delight them. Also, interact with your followers by commenting and liking their content. In this way, you bond with them on a higher level and you look like an accessible and realistic brand type that is a good addition to your positive image. Another thing to keep in mind is the number of people who follow you and the number of people you follow. For example, if you follow 1000 people and 200 of them follow you, it looks sad. We're not saying you should stop following people but take care of who you're following. If you follow all the people who liked your photo, regardless of their real interests, the result will be the same.

TRAFFIC

As we mentioned in the first part of this list, you can put a link to your biography description. Brands often forget about it completely, which is a big mistake. In this situation, followers have to "search" for you on Google and that's just what they don't want to do. Trust us: people are lazy. If you have the opportunity to publish a link to your website, it makes sense to use it. The link in the biography should always be in your mind and you can play with it. If you have some kind of blog and publish regularly, take a photo or video, put a link in your biography and tell your followers that they can find a link to a blog in the biography. That way, it will intrigue them and make them want to read it, which is exactly what you want them to do. This also applies to products. If you have a product in your webshop that you would like to present to your followers so that they go to your webshop and take a look at other products as well, create content and direct them to the link in the biography. There are many possibilities to play with, and we recommend using them. Sometimes it's not the best solution to attract followers to your website if you haven't had time to optimize it. However, we recommend having a link to your website in the biography, no matter how it looks, because, you know, it's easier for followers to explore your brand. In this case, avoid publishing the previously mentioned content and highlight your website until you really optimize it.

HOW TO CORRECTLY USE #HASHTAGS IN INSTAGRAM?

As I mentioned earlier, hashtags are an essential and powerful tool of Instagram. It is derived from another social network, Twitter, and Instagram introduced them a little later. Nowadays it is difficult to find images without their description or comments containing at least some hashtags. Why are hashtags important? Well, because that's one of the ways you can attract people to your content. To ensure that these people are your target audience, you must use hashtags wisely and carefully. We will try to give you some basic tips on how you can govern Instagram and attract the right people to your Instagram profile using the right hashtags. First of all, before you start talking about hashtags, you should be careful to set up your public profile. If it's private, the whole concept with hashtags doesn't make any sense because your content won't appear in any search results. Now that we've made it clear, you must know what is possible and what not to write in the form of hashtags. For example, you can type numbers, but signs such as money signs (\$ or €) will not appear in the search result. You can write up to 30 hashtags, which, of course, doesn't mean you have to. However, there are also some forbidden hashtags, which you should be careful not to use. Most of them are understandable because they contain inappropriate words, but beware of words that are not so logical, for example, #popular or #like. The best way is to try to find some hashtags you want to use. If you can't find anything, it means that the hashtag is forbidden or doesn't exist. Besides, it's great because if you run into a lot of boring pictures, you better skip that hashtag.

THE MORE SPECIFIC, THE BETTER!

If it's a company that, say, sells furniture, it won't use the hashtag as #food. That's pretty obvious. Even so, there are some people who write down absolutely everything that comes to mind just to appear in every search result. That's definitely the wrong approach because you want to attract people who are looking for something you can really provide. Of course, if you sell furniture, you can provide people with beds, closets, mirrors, etc. However, the fact that you can offer them that does not mean that I should put it all into your hashtags. Why? Because you need to attract people who are looking for something at that moment. That means they're likely to buy something because they need it right now. If in the image you have a sofa and underneath it, you write all the products you have, the people who look for beds and see the sofa will not be happy. We understand that you want them to know that you have all that, but you won't take it anywhere because you won't continue with the next step. Instead, you should try to be as specific as you can. You need to put yourself in the buyer's place. What kind of couch do you want? By adding a few adjectives, you can narrow your search and get the target audience that will surely be interested in your product. For example, the sofa is yellow, so add #yellowsofa. There aren't many people looking for it, but whoever it is, they'll come across your photo and be the right audience. Therefore, hashtags must be meaningful and a good representation of what is really in the image.

CUSTOM HASHTAGS

Many companies write their name as a hashtag, which is fine if your company has an attractive short name. If not, it is better to shorten it in some way or use your company's slogan or saying. Here at Kontra, we like to combine it, so we are using #kontraagency and #turningthingsaround. It must be coherent for it to spread and be recognizable. In addition, because you can follow people and brands on Instagram, you can also follow hashtags, which makes it easier for your target audience to stay up to date with everything you publish with that particular hashtag.

CONSULT YOUR OPTIONS

You can do some research before deciding which hashtags you want to use. One of the best ways to examine that could be by searching for different hashtags. For example, if you are going to put #business when describing your image, you can first look up this hashtag and observe what people wrote next to it. It can be # success, maybe # work, etc. That way, you can better understand the interests of your target audience. You don't need to concentrate only on customers; you can broaden your search in your competition as well. See if they are already using the same hashtags you want to use. If they're more successful, you might end up in the shadows. That's why you need to find other variations of the same thing.

INTELLIGENT, NOT POPULAR

If you look for hashtags on the web, I'm sure you'll find different sites that will give you a lot of hashtag ideas, even sorted by topic. These sites have the ability to copy these hashtags, so you don't have to think too much. Don't do that! These hashtags are typical, wide and will take you nowhere. If you're just copying and pasting popular hashtags, maybe you'll get a lot of likes in this particular publication, but it won't be from the right people and you won't get followers forever. It's best to try to think of something innovative, catchy, something that can define your brand, not something irrelevant.

COMBINE AND TEST

You can try different hashtags, try them and see which ones give you the best results. In addition, you can put hashtags both in your subtitle and in the first comment. Basically, these two forms have the same function, but sometimes it seems to be full of too many hashtags in the title, so it's best to put it in the comments. You can even experiment with this by using only a few crucial hashtags that want to be visible in the title and then add the rest in the first comment. You should always follow your industry trends so you can use them in your hashtags. However, these are some basic things you should follow if you want your Instagram profile to be professional. However, everything else is up to you. So, combine, try, and of course have fun!

INSTAGRAM STORIES: HOW TO USE THEM AND WHY?

There was Snapchat with its missing content and ingenious filters for selfies, but then came the summer of 2016 and Instagram presents Stories as its response to Snapchat. The rest is history: Instagram stories are now more popular than Snapchat. I mean, of course: when Instagram presented Stories for the first time, everyone talked about how they copied Snapchat. In addition, there were many complaints of how this will ruin the Instagram experience for people. None of these turned out to be true. Firstly, Instagram did not copy Snapchat: they improved their idea and made it their own. Basically, they created a better version that was easier to use for both ordinary people and businesses. There was no need to address two different applications; instead, you could plan your content in the same application, both for the regular Instagram feed and for Stories.

Obviously, many vendors were confused at first about how to use Instagram to their advantage in their business. Here's the thing: Instagram was never for you. Before Stories, before announcing it in Instagram, before all that, there was only a simple idea that Instagram existed as a simple and fun application to share people's favorite moments with their friends in the form of a polaroid-shaped image. Its popularity has grown, and companies have realized that. Suddenly, they showed up there too. And people didn't care, as they were used to communicating with them on Facebook. In addition, Instagram allowed companies to communicate with their target audience in a different way than Facebook. Years have passed and many things have changed. If you don't pay attention, you won't be able to keep up with the constantly changing Instagram game rules. There is an ongoing conversation about shadowban (for those who don't know, shadowban hides its Instagram posts from users who don't follow it, which means that, if you block Instagram and use hashtags in your posts, only you and your current group of followers will see them when they search for the hashtags you used: this removes your commitment and prevents you from getting new followers.

WHY COMPANIES SHOULD USE INSTAGRAM STORIES

Not enough companies use Insta Stories. The first reason is because they don't understand them. Many companies have a couple of board members who understand that any normal and modern company in the 21st century needs to have a social networking strategy, but everyone wants to see the numbers, KPIs, purchases that their social networking publications brought them, and so on. So how do you explain to them that a portion of their social media budget should be invested in Insta Stories, which makes difficult-to-measure content disappear in something other than a number of people who saw that content? Another thing is that many companies still don't have internal digital departments or marketing experts who understand social networks and usually outsource that part to some agency. But if you're working in a digital agency, you know you can't really publish anything on your own and you should check everything with your client to make sure they're okay with the content, the message you're trying to communicate, and so on. The stories of Instagram must be instantaneous. Something that happened right now, right now, right this second.

Obviously, you can't just publish it before you send it to the client and then they have to approve it, which can take time if they haven't seen an email or if they want to make some changes. You understand what I'm trying to say. The point is, this doesn't work. You must explain to them that they will simply have to believe you will do everything in your power to create the best content for them and in their best interest. Trends in Instagram change daily. That's why you won't be able to stick to your monthly plan all the time. Insta Stories are as important as the content published in a normal feed. In fact, my instinct tells me that Insta Stories will be the biggest trend this year with more and more people (and companies!) Using them, they provide a real and direct connection with their followers and help them get to know you and your company better. While your artistic photos, which you carefully edited and formulated for your feed, will bring you new followers and showcase your products, services or whatever you publish, Stories will give your existing followers a more accurate view of what is happening behind the scenes. Even more so because regular Instagram publications are subject to the sometimes fickle Instagram algorithm, but Instagram will not penalize you for publishing too many Instagram Stories.

Do you need ideas for what to publish on your Stories? How about tips and tricks on how to use your product? Or inspiring ideas on how your product helped others? Or take a look at the new product you're launching to promote it? Show them how to use your product or how practical it is, what benefits they will have if they use it... The possibilities are endless. In short, Instagram stories are a great way to build your brand, build a stronger relationship with your audience, provide them with valuable content, interact with them and increase awareness. The stories are presented at the top of

Instagram and are one of the best ways to increase engagement and visibility among your followers. The most important thing is that Instagram Stories are a rather relaxed place in comparison with the regular photos and videos published in the feed, and the quality standards are much lower than those of the regular publications. It means you shouldn't be afraid to post something silly: A funny Boomerang from your team to have drinks after work, for example!

HOW TO USE INSTAGRAM STORIES

Let's be honest, the world is your oyster since Instagram created so many great tools for Stories that you can use live videos, Rewing, Boomerang, 15-second videos, Zoom option, Surveys, filters, hashtags, stickers, location, labeling, etc. But if that's not enough for you, there are other applications you can use to make your Insta Stories really stand out. For example, download Canva to upload your photos in its amazing designs and eye-catching templates! Want to add animated text to your content? Don't worry, the Legend application has it covered. For iOS, I suggest Hype Type. If you want to make music, add text and more to your Insta Stories, then play the InShot app (available for both Android and iOS). If you want your Instagram Stories to contain more than a simple vertical image or video, use PicPlayPost (again, available on iOS and Android). It's a perfect application for creating photo collages and video ready to share. Want to add some shine to your Insta Stories?

Consider downloading Kirakira + (only in iOS) Want to plan your Insta stories in advance? The preview application makes it easier! See how many options? All you need to do is be creative and keep up with all the Instagram trends (because there are so many). Easy, isn't it? Don't panic, once you get into it, you'll see how amazing it can be.

Best Practices

I'm not going to mention the Instagram ads (which are available in Stories, as well as in the normal feed). Although they allow you to link them directly to your website, blog or web shop, I want you to concentrate entirely on creating the best possible Insta Stories in a completely organic way. So, my first advice for you is to tell a story. It may seem obvious, but you'll be surprised how many brands don't follow this advice or, even worse, don't know how to use Insta Stories to tell their story. Stories are great for telling stories (see what I did there?). Your Instagram strategy should not be just a bunch of randomly chosen images. All of these elements must play well together to tell a complete story of your business. All of these individual pieces of content should be pieces of a larger puzzle. Although Insta Stories are pieces of a puzzle that will disappear, they can still have an impact. That's why it's so important to be authentic. Be fun, informative, and engaging. Keep your content perfectly polished for your feed publications. In Stories, be as creative and whimsical as possible, but don't forget to provide value.

Your content, in feed or Stories, won't have value if you don't make sure your content will bring viewers back for more. Instagram Stories are designed for content that appears to have been captured (even if it wasn't). You can and should plan ahead, but don't expect to be able to do it every time. In the meantime, some new trends may appear and will have to adapt. And adaptability is crucial for creating incredible content for your Insta Stories. Continue reading? Good for you. So, remember when I suggested some ideas for content you can share on Insta Stories earlier? Well, here are some examples along with an account of how to do it right.

1. Instruction Tutorial

Great idea for a series of Insta Stories. Show people how to use your product and what they can do with it: for your base of craft-loving followers, create attractive insta stories with step-by-step instructions on creative projects.

2. Behind the scenes: Do you have a web shop and you're preparing to launch a new collection of products? Excellent! While there are months left before the official launch, show your fans behind the scenes by posting a couple of videos from the photo shoot to give them an idea of what they can expect to see in this upcoming

collection. That way, it will promote them and make them want to pre-order it. Oui Fresh makes amazing stories behind the scenes of Insta!

3. Does everyone love the Top 10 Best Selling Lists on your website? The Top 10 Most Read Posts on your blog? List of the Best Booked Apartments in your hotel? List of the best books you've read this month? All the great ideas to share in a couple of Urges Stories to your followers! It's informative and fun, but it can also be inspiring and engaging. Just what you want and need. See how Bookworm Boutique does it

4. Questions and Answers or Surveys: Time to start the conversation! Insta Stories allow you to get feedback from your followers, so why not ask them anything and everything that interests you? For example, Taco Bell regularly asks its audience what type of content they would like to see on the Instagram brands. You can take a survey and choose between two options or you can, for example, ask your followers what your company's favorite product is and publish it in their Insta Stories while tagging it. That way, you will receive comments, but also visibility, as they will share your products with their followers, label you and possibly bring you new followers.

CONCLUSION

I hope you found this path a very attractive one. This way of producing Instagram content is very profitable for your personal brand or any brand you want to market. I invite you to pursue all your ideals wherever you go and tell people how you are doing so through Instagram. I hope that all this we are talking about has helped you to improve on your way to success. Check the bundle we have on all three volumes. See you at the peak of success.